Michael Pike

Effective
Church
Planning

P/33 - Left or Right Brained

Effective Church Planning

Lyle E. Schaller

Abingdon
Nashville

EFFECTIVE CHURCH PLANNING

Copyright © 1979 by Abingdon

Library of Congress Cataloging in Publication Data

SCHALLER, LYLE E
  Effective church planning.
  1. Church management. I. Title.
BV652.5.S32   658'.91'25   78-26462

ISBN 0-687-11530-2

Portions of this book are based on material which first appeared in these periodicals. Grateful acknowledgement is made to the following publications:
Review of Religious Research for "Human Ethology: The Most Neglected Factors in Church Planning," vol. 17, Fall 1975. Copyright 1975, by The Religious Research Association, Inc.
Learning With, for "Why Is Mary Hunter Unhappy?" September 1976. Copyright 1976 Augsburg Publishing House and the Board of Publication of the Lutheran Church in America.
Church Administration, for "Winners or Losers?" May 1977. Copyright, The Sunday School Board of the Southern Baptist Convention.
The Christian Century, for "Dr. Schlesinger's Threshing Machine" October 12, 1977. Copyright 1977 by the Christian Century Foundation. All rights reserved under the International Copyright Union, the Universal Copyright Convention, and the Pan-American Copyright Convention.

MANUFACTURED BY THE PARTHENON PRESS AT
NASHVILLE, TENNESSEE, UNITED STATES OF AMERICA

To
William J. Grossman
Bryant M. Kirkland

Contents

Effective Church Planning

Introduction

"Tonight marks the end of your first year here, and tomorrow will be the first day of your second year as our pastor," observed Bill Kirkland as he and Mrs. Kirkland entertained the pastor and his wife at dinner one evening. "What are your reflections on this first year?"

"To be honest with you, I guess it's a mixed bag," replied the thirty-eight-year-old minister, who was completing the first year of his third pastorate. "Part of it may be a result of the fact that this is a much larger congregation than I've ever served before. On the plus side, despite my failure to get people to move down and sit in those front pews, I enjoy preaching to larger crowds than I ever have before, and I'm highly impressed with the dedication of many of the leaders here such as you and Emily. I also appreciate having a full-time secretary for the first time. Most of all, I guess I feel good about most of the members' willingness to consider new ideas and to try new ministries. I also believe this church has the potential for substantial growth. There are a lot of unchurched people out there that we could and should be reaching with the Gospel.

"On the other side of the ledger, I am dismayed at the almost complete inactivity of nearly a fourth of our members, the part-time religion of another larger percentage of the people, including some of the Board members who rarely attend Board meetings. I also feel frustrated by the presence of two or three cliques where the primary allegiance of the members seems to be to their class or group, rather than to Jesus Christ and the church.

"When I was contemplating coming here, I was attracted by the opportunity I thought I saw to work with small groups, but I haven't had much time to do that yet, and the results haven't been very impressive thus far. Two or three of our adult classes are far more attached to the room they meet in than to the goal of learning more about their faith. Despite everything I've tried, I'm still depressed by the lack of joy among some of our church school teachers. I believe they should get more joy out of teaching. Perhaps my biggest problem thus far is the attitude of three or four men on the trustees and the finance committee who are so opposed to innovation. That may be because they want a strong leader, and I see myself more as an enabler.

"Finally, one of the reasons I was interested in coming here was that this is a university town, and I thought a part of my time would be spent as a minister to students. I've discovered, however, that is a far different and more difficult ministry than I had expected."

This book is directed at the issues this frustrated pastor has raised in the conversation with one of his members. If we look more carefully at his comments, it becomes apparent that his reflections are focused primarily on symptoms rather than on the basic issues. In one sense that is the basic theme of this volume. Why does it happen that way? What are the underlying factors that have a low visibility but a high impact on the dynamics of the life of the parish? What are the institutional factors that often are neglected, but frequently are very influential in determining the course of ecclesiastical events?

The basic assumption on which this book is based is that nearly all people have a far greater capability than they believe they have to resolve problems and to respond creatively to complex issues *if they have an accurate diagnosis of the nature of the situation.* Frequently the basic cause of frustration is not in the problem itself, but rather in the attempt to respond to clichés and symptoms rather than to the central issue.

The pedagogical style, to use an ominous term, used in presenting the material in this volume is to encourage reflection on specific and relatively common questions. The expectation is that when the reader's experiences and reflections are combined with the printed word, this will produce new understandings about what is happening and why it is happening that way.

The first and longest chapter is an effort to identify and analyze one of the most widely neglected factors in working with people. *Many of the techniques, methods, and procedures that are used to facilitate the dynamics of small groups are counterproductive when used with large groups.* One result is that normal human beings do not want to sit in the front pews when a large group of people gather for corporate worship. This is one of many distinctions between the nature of small groups and the dynamics of large groups that are identified in the first chapter.

The attachment of human beings to places and to the relationships with other persons has been overlooked by those persons who tend to take a professional, "logical," rational, unemotional, and functional view of the world. Why this perspective tends to be self-defeating is examined in the second chapter. This difference in perspective is also one of the major components of the widely discussed lay-clergy gap.

One of the reasons many people respond to any new idea with the exclamation, "We could never do that here!" is that this reaction is a natural product of the allocative approach to planning. The choice of the planning model to be used has a tremendous impact on the nature of the recommendations that emerge from any planning effort. That widely neglected fact of life is the central theme of the third chapter, which suggests alternative planning models for more creative results.

The natural human tendency to focus on symptoms, rather than to diagnose the basic underlying issues, is the theme of the brief fourth chapter. While this emphasis on diagnosis is a central theme of the entire book, this chapter illustrates the point with four very common examples from congregational experiences.

The unnecessarily unhappy and joyless Sunday school teacher is the subject of the fifth chapter. This chapter also suggests (a) why any single-factor analysis of a problem frequently is incomplete, (b) how the diagnosis may be very complex in what appear to be simple problems, (c) why the basic distinction between visual and verbal communication is an increasingly important subject in church planning, and (d) a few constructive responses to the problem.

Many congregations excel in motivating people by guilt. The sixth chapter identifies several of the more widely used methods for doing this and for creating low morale. It also offers suggestions on alternatives and healthier methods for motivating people.

For many years the enabler style of pastoral leadership has been held up to seminarians and to ministers as the ideal approach. After years of parish experience with the concept, the time has arrived to examine why this may be an impossible challenge for the overwhelming majority of pastors. That is the theme of the seventh, and what may turn out to be the most controversial chapter in this volume.

Another perspective for understanding the purpose of this volume is to reflect on a little-used term, *biotic potential*. The dictionary defines this as the capacity for a population to increase in number under optimum environmental conditions. Many congregations today are making church growth their number one goal. To facilitate the attainment of this goal it helps to look at the organizational content and to identify the factors which (a) encourage the attraction, reception, and assimilation of new members and (b) inhibit the capability of that congregation for growth. In an earlier volume (*Assimilating New Members*, Abingdon, 1978), I wrote to the first half of that two-part formula. The focus in this volume is on identifying and analyzing some of the neglected institutional environmental factors in a congregation that tend to inhibit the personal and spiritual growth of the members and block the numerical growth of the congregation. Using small group procedures in working with large groups of people, ignoring the importance of place in people's lives, using an allocative planning approach, treating symptoms rather than working on problems, neglecting the basic causes of the unhappiness of lay volunteers, using guilt to motivate people, and unintentionally creating low morale—these are some of the counterproductive behavior patterns that inhibit the life, ministry, and outreach of a congregation. All these, and other similar factors

14

are discussed in this volume. What are the factors influencing the biotic potential of your congregation?

Every book has many authors, and this one is no exception to that generalization. I am indebted to many lay leaders, pastors, students, and friends for their insights and suggestions. The limitations of space and memory make it impossible to list them all by name. There are, however, two persons who deserve a special word of thanks. In a casual conversation in Toronto, Bill Lord of The United Church of Canada planted the seed that grew into the first chapter. My friend David first made me aware of the concept of biotic potential.

Finally, this volume is dedicated to two friends, who by both word and deed place preaching where it belongs on the priority scale, at the very top.

1

Small Groups and Large Groups

"When I came here a year ago, I thought I was coming to an exceptionally well-organized congregation, built around a major emphasis on small groups," reflected the Reverend Everett Hamlin to his friend Jerry Smith, who was the pastor of a nearby church. "I have always felt very comfortable working with small groups, so I was especially attracted to the possibilities here at Trinity. Now that I've been here awhile, I find I was misled. I don't know whether it was intentional or not, but this church isn't organized around small groups, they have factions! It's organized as three congregations, and I'm seen as the head of one congregation and viewed as an outsider by the other two."

"I don't quite follow you," questioned Jerry Smith. "What do you mean when you say congregations and factions?"

"I really don't know which is the better word to use," replied Everett. "First, there is the congregation I preach to on Sunday morning. I think I'm clearly the accepted leader of that group of people, and I feel very comfortable with them. Second, there's the Sunday school, which has a very strong adult division and four huge adult classes. Each of those is almost a little congregation in itself, with its own teacher, its own treasury and treasurer, its own room, its own mission project, its own prayer list, its own series of monthly social events, and its own private agenda. When I was in seminary, I was taught to organize Sunday school classes around small groups of seven to fifteen people, but the smallest of these

17

four adult classes has an average attendance of nearly thirty. What really gets me, I guess, is that they violate nearly every rule I've been taught about how small groups should function. I tried to persuade the two smallest classes to meet with their chairs in a big circle so the people could see each other, which would facilitate dialog, but they insisted on lining the chairs up in a military formation so the members of the class are looking at the backs of people's heads, rather than at each other. Yet, somehow, each class is a very tightly knit and cohesive group.

"The third slice of the picture is the women's organization," continued Everett Hamlin, his frustration becoming more obvious as he expressed his pent-up feelings. "In my previous church the women's organization had about forty active members, and they were divided into four circles which met once a month as study groups with eight to ten women in each. I met the first week of the month with the four study group leaders. We went over that month's lesson very carefully, and I trained them to lead their groups in studying that lesson. At Trinity there are about one hundred and fifty women actively involved, and they're also divided into four circles. Each circle has an attendance of twenty-five to thirty each month, but there the resemblance stops. Each circle picks its own theme and does its own thing. One is a traditional Bible study group, one is a crafts group that has no study, one is a strictly social fellowship group of young mothers, and one is a social action group. In addition, they have general meetings every month with fifty or sixty women present, put on a big ham dinner every spring, and have a huge bazaar every October. I never have learned how much money they take in, but it must be around $5,000 or $6,000 a year. Once a year they ask the pastor to take the program for a monthly general meeting, and that's about all I have to do with it."

"Obviously you're not happy about all of this," interrupted Jerry Smith in a mild tone of voice, "but I'm not clear on what it is that disturbs you."

"I'll tell you what bugs me," replied his frustrated friend. "I came here thinking I was coming to a much larger congregation that was organized around a large number of strong small groups and that wanted a minister who was comfortable working with small groups. Instead of that, I find myself the pastor of a large collection of people divided into three congregations, the Sunday morning worshiping congregation, the Sunday school organization, and the women's congregation. They're not organized around small groups, they're organized into three political parties."

"And part of what bothers you," said Jerry Smith, "is that two of those political parties act as if they don't need you. Is that part of the picture?"

The frustration expressed by Everett Hamlin is not simply a result of feeling unneeded and unwanted by the adult Sunday school classes and the women's organization at Trinity. That is really a symptom of a more complex issue which is one of the most widely neglected factors in church planning. In academic terms the issue is the distinction between primary groups and large formal organizations. At Trinity Church the recently arrived pastor was attempting to conceptualize the programmatic structure in terms of primary groups, but in fact the core of the program was structured around large formal organizations. Part of Everett Hamlin's frustration resulted from his failure to grasp this distinction. Part of his frustration resulted from his effort to apply small group techniques to the management of large groups. He had been misinformed that Trinity was organized around small primary groups. No one had helped him understand that many of the techniques and approaches that can be very helpful in strengthening the life and functioning of small groups are often counterproductive when applied to large formal organizations.

Before moving to a discussion of these differences, it may be helpful to illustrate the same point by looking at what can happen in the administrative (as contrasted with the programmatic) structure of a congregation.

"I can't put my finger on the reason, but it seems to me that ever since this new pastor arrived, I go home from these Board meetings feeling a high level of frustration," declared Joe Ferrell to his friend, Al Williams, as they walked out to the parking lot at eleven-fifteen one June evening. "It used to be our Board ran very smoothly, and we would be through in two hours. Now we sit around and bicker for three or four hours and don't get as much done as we used to accomplish in half the time. Unless things change, I can tell you now this will be my last year on the Board."

"The length of our meetings is only a part of the reason for your frustration, Joe," responded Al Williams. "A bigger factor is that this new pastor is attempting to use small group techniques with a 36-member Board, and it won't work. If you remember, when we interviewed him, he said he felt his number one competence was working with small groups. I think he was right. He has all of the techniques of managing small groups down pat. The reason you and I feel so frustrated is that most of those techniques are counterproductive when they are applied to a large group such as our Board."

"Well, I'm glad to know you share my feelings of frustration," replied a puzzled Joe Ferrell, "but I don't know what in the world you're talking about. I think I understood every word you said, but I didn't understand any of the sentences. Would you please try that over again in simple language that I can understand? I hear you saying the new pastor is the reason for our frustration with Board meetings, but I don't understand this small group–large group business.

"I can tell you another thing that frustrates me, however," continued Joe. "It used to be that we functioned as one Board, the focus was on the business before the Board, everyone was there when we were ready to begin, we started on time, we stuck to the agenda, everybody paid attention, and we got the job done in two hours. Occasionally someone would suddenly mention that we only had ten minutes until adjournment, and I would wonder what had happened, the time had gone so fast. Now people straggle in, we rarely begin on time, an hour later there is a little two-person conversation going on down at that end of the room, a couple of people are holding their own private committee meeting over there, three or four have gone out to the kitchen to get a cup of coffee, and we have to call everybody back together when we want to vote on something. Now we operate like a bunch of United States Senators, not like a Church Board!"

SMALL GROUPS AND LARGE GROUPS

The conflict identified by Joe and Al parallels the source of Everett Hamlin's frustration at Trinity Church. The issue is one of the basic, and also one of the three or four most neglected, factors in planning and administering the life and program of the worshiping congregation. It is the same issue that helps to explain why people prefer not to sit in the front pews at worship; why the small congregation, averaging twenty-five or thirty at worship, can be very comfortable in a building designed to seat ninety for worship, but the congregation with a hundred present feels uncomfortably small when worshiping in a building designed to seat three hundred; why many of the older ladies in the women's organization object to shifting the membership of the circles every year or two; why the seating arrangement should be radically different for a meeting of a ten-person governing board than for the meeting of a forty-member board or council; why the larger congregations often want a stronger initiating style of ministerial leadership than do smaller churches; why name-tags are so important in large congregations seeking to grow in size; why considerable time often is spent on introductions in small groups, but not in large groups; and why the choir in particular and the music program in general is of increasing importance as the size of a congregation climbs upward. To respond creatively to these and many related questions that keep coming up in the ongoing life of the worshiping congregation it is necessary to recognize the basic differences between large groups and small groups!

During the past three or four decades a tremendous quantity of insights, wisdom, skills, techniques, models, experiences, and knowledge has been accumulated about nurturing the life of the small group of five to fifteen persons.[1] Although there is a lack of universal agreement on the definition of "small," most authorities agree that the maximum size of a small group is twelve to seventeen persons, and the point of diminishing returns is reached when a group includes more than seventeen persons. When a group includes twenty to thirty or more individuals, the dynamics change, and it no longer qualifies as a small group. Much of this wisdom and knowledge about the dynamics of small groups has been introduced into the churches and is widely utilized by

21

ministers, educational specialists, youth counselors, and lay leaders.

By contrast, a comparatively small quantity of wisdom, insights, and knowledge has been accumulated about the management of large groups that include more than a score of people. Relatively little of this wisdom and knowledge has been introduced to the churches. This failure of the leaders in the churches to (a) recognize the distinction between large groups and small groups and (b) use different procedures in working with large groups has had some negative results.

Five Points of Frustration

One result of neglecting this basic distinction in working with groups of different sizes is that many churches are attempting to use small-group techniques and skills in managing large groups, and the results are counterproductive with frustration, a disappointing level of participation, a leveling off or plateauing in the growth pattern, internal conflict, and a high dropout rate among the major products of that misdirected effort.

A second result is that many pastors have been attempting to use small group techniques in organizing the life of large (two hundred or more members) congregations, with the result being there is no effective group life for one-half to four-fifths of the members.

A third result is that many pastors specializing in small-group techniques literally become "overworked" when the congregation passes the two-hundred-member mark. This usually produces an exhausted pastor, a neglected pastor's spouse, a disproportionately large number of inactive members, and a ceiling on the growth potential of that congregation (see item 17, page 44).

A fourth result has been to bring the concept of "process" into disrepute. The process used in managing small groups has many valuable characteristics, some of which are absolutely essential to the creation and maintenance of continuing, meaningful and effective small groups. When these process techniques are applied to the management of large groups of people, the results are often counterproductive. Instead of recognizing the error was in attempting to apply the wrong management techniques, a more common recent response has been to denounce "process management."[2]

Finally, the pastor who is highly skilled in the application of small group techniques and applies them effectively in the small or middle-sized congregation may experience considerable frustration after moving to a large congregation where the appropriate ministerial leadership style requires an emphasis on working with large formal organizations. This is what happened to Everett Hamlin, and a few of the results of that mismatch are described in the opening paragraphs of this chapter.

Before looking in more detail at the implications of the differences between large groups and small groups, it may be helpful to define the basic terms.

What Is Small?

In broad general terms a small group varies from as few as two or three individuals to as many as fifteen to seventeen. Several studies indicate that the quality of the interaction among the members of a small group reaches an optimum point when (a) the group is composed of an odd, rather than an even number of people, (b) the group includes five or seven persons, (c) the group has a clearly identified leader, (d) that leader has a high level of competence in leading small groups, (e) the meeting place is of the appropriate size for the group, (f) everyone feels free to participate actively in group discussions, and (g) the members do not feel compelled to engage in what to some of them is excessive participation—a point reached with five or seven persons.[3]

There are many other variables influencing the optimum size of a small group. These include the temperature and the quality of the air at the meeting place, the quality of the meeting place, the age and sex of the participants, the nature of the task given the group, the degree of success in accomplishing that task, the amount of time the members have been together, the frequency of meetings, the length of the meetings, the skill of the group leader in responding to the expectations the members have for that leader, the degree of heterogeneity among the members of the group, the skills of the members in fulfilling their responsibilities in that group, whether the organizational structure of the group is appropriate for the reasons for that group's existence, the influence of kinship ties, and the degree of competitiveness among the members.

In discussing the size of groups it should be noted that it is possible to develop what are in effect, overgrown small groups. These display most of the characteristics of the cohesive and unified group of twelve to fifteen persons, but the actual number of members is far larger. Examples of this include the small congregation that has had thirty to thirty-five persons at worship for decades; the baseball squad of two dozen players who have played together every day for two or three seasons and have just won the championship; the seven-year-old congregation of eighty-five members, most of whom have been members for at least four or five years; the thirty-two survivors of the army company who have just returned from three weeks of intensive fighting; and the twenty-nine-member adult Sunday school class that, with the exception of one new member who joined the class eight years ago, has been together for a quarter of a century. These groups function in a manner similar to the small group of twelve to fifteen members, but include more people. The basic internal dynamics are the same as for the typical small group, but the number of members is far larger. These groups represent an important exception to the basic generalizations presented in this chapter.

These examples of "large small groups" also illustrate the simple fact of life that the internal dynamics of groups are not exclusively a function of size. In general, the characteristics of a group change as the size moves into double digits, and usually most of the unique characteristics of the small group disappear or change when the number of members reaches seventeen or eighteen or nineteen or twenty, but there are exceptions. It is extremely important for the person working with small groups to be aware of the exceptions.

Although the overgrown small groups display many of the

24

internal dynamics of the typical small group of ten to fifteen persons, their cohesiveness usually becomes more fragile if and when the size of the group increases sharply, they usually find it more difficult to accept and assimilate a few additional new members, and they display some of the characteristics of large groups.

The basic generalization to remember in understanding the influence of size on the dynamics of a group, however, is not a numerical cutoff point that automatically distinguishes small groups from large groups. A better analogy is a spectrum with the typical small groups of three, four, five, or seven members represented at the left end of the spectrum. At the left-center of the spectrum are the groups with seven to twelve members. In the middle of this spectrum are the groups with twelve to seventeen or eighteen members. At the right of the center are the groups of twenty to forty persons, which are basically large groups, but some of them are overgrown small groups and display several of the characteristics of small groups, and these may overshadow their basic characteristics as large groups. Scattered along the right quarter of this spectrum are the groups that range in size from thirty to forty members to several hundred people. The larger the number of people, the greater the probability that small-group techniques and methods will be counterproductive if they are used by the leader(s) in working with that collection of individuals.

In this discussion the term *small group* refers to the internal dynamics typical of the group that includes fewer than twelve to seventeen persons. (Mark 14 suggests that when a group includes as many as twelve or thirteen people, the only dynamic the leader can count on is that one member of the group will betray him and another will deny he ever knew him.) The term *large group* refers to those occasions when twenty to forty or more individuals are gathered together with the expectation they will function as a cohesive and unified group. The larger the number of people, the more likely that group will behave in predictable large-group patterns.

Now, what are those differences between the behavior patterns of small groups and large groups? For both illustrative and instructive purposes it may be helpful to identify a range of differences, but the length of this list should not mislead anyone into assuming it is offered as an exhaustive statement of the differences.

What Makes the Difference?

(1.) The first, and perhaps the most highly visible, difference between small groups and large groups is in the seating arrangements. In a small group the primary focus usually, but not always, is on the members of the group. Therefore one of the means of reinforcing this is to arrange the chairs in a circle facing inward to enable each participant to see the other members of the group, to maximize eye contact, to facilitate conversation, to give visibility to nonverbal communication, and to encourage active participation. (If the primary purpose of the gathering is "business," the use of tables will facilitate the process. If the primary purpose of the gathering is the interpersonal relationships among the members of that group, it is better to avoid the use of tables.) This ideal seating arrangement for a small group can be accomplished easily and effectively with groups of two to seven persons. The circle, or square, of chairs becomes a less influential asset when the number of participants passes seven, and when the group includes fifteen to twenty or more persons, the disadvantages of the large circle begin to offset the advantages. Members of the group begin to feel frustrated that they cannot maintain eye contact with everyone, some of the nonverbal communication is lost, small subgroups of two or three persons begin to form spontaneously at the edges of the cluster as time passes, the leader has difficulty holding the attention of some of the participants, and fatigue usually becomes obvious after forty or fifty minutes.

By contrast, in arranging the seating of a large group, the focus should be on the group's agenda, the reason for gathering or the nature of the group. This may be accomplished by use of a pulpit, a communion table, an altar, a cross, a speaker's platform, a stage, newsprint on the wall, an easel, a chalkboard, a flag, banners, icons, a painting, a projection screen, a central display, a large

26

printed agenda hung on the wall, a brilliantly lighted area, or a speaker's table. The rest of the seats are arranged so the persons attending will have their attention focused on that central point which represents the reason they came together. The greater the number of people and/or the larger the proportion of persons who do not know other members of that group, the more important it becomes to physically focus the attention of those present on the agenda, or the reason for coming together.

Perhaps the most neglected factor in understanding this distinction between the best seating arrangements for a small group and the appropriate seating arrangement for a large group of people concerns the quality or attractiveness of particular places to sit.

In a small group the best seats are the front seats. Active involvement in the interaction among the members of the group is facilitated by a front row seat. Anyone who sits in the second circle of chairs in a group composed of four or five or six or seven people in the inner circle and a like number in the outer circles feels like an outsider or a spectator or a nonparticipant or an alien or a secondary figure. In a small group, where the primary focus is on the interaction of the participants, the best seats are in those places which facilitate participation in the interaction.

By contrast, in a large group where the primary focus is on the speaker or the program or the business agenda or the entertainment or the presentation of material, rather than on the interaction of people, the worst seats are the front seats (these seats blur the distinction between spectator and participant) and the best seats are (a) the rear seats next to the back wall and/or the end seats next to the aisle and/or those seats closest to the exit. In terms of group dynamics the opposite of participation is departure, and the seats which offer the opportunity for an easy and unobtrusive departure are better seats than the relatively conspicuous front row seats.

Furthermore, the active participants in a small group are willing to make the tradeoff of having a few people seated behind them in order to benefit from the advantages of those front seats. By contrast, most of the members of a large group have a more passive role in what is happening and therefore prefer to see rather than to be seen. For them, the more favorable tradeoff is to sit toward the back where they can survey the entire scene, be relatively inconspicuous, have access to an unobtrusive exit, and be partially removed from the focal point of that event.

Why do most people persist in sitting on the back pews during Sunday morning worship? Why do they insist on sitting on the aisle, although this will inconvenience latecomers, who must squeeze past them to the vacant place near the center of that pew? They do this because this is normal behavior for members of a large group!

This distinction between the seating arrangements for small groups and large groups also can be illustrated by two other examples. The small rural congregation with two dozen people gathering for worship on the average Sunday can meet in a building seating one hundred without feeling overwhelmed by the empty pews, because the primary focus of the people is on the members of the group, not on the meeting place. By contrast, when one hundred people gather for worship in a sanctuary seating three hundred, they feel discouraged by the large number of empty pews, since the focus of the people is more on the place than on the group.

When a committee of seven or eight or nine individuals gather for their monthly business meeting, they usually will be very comfortable when seated around two tables that are pushed together with two or three chairs on each of the four sides. It is not disruptive for the pastor to sit on one side, for the person chairing the meeting to sit opposite the pastor, for the person speaking most frequently to sit on a third side, while the member displaying printed materials may sit on the fourth side of the square.

By contrast, however, in that same congregation a radically different seating arrangement is appropriate when the monthly meeting of the 42-member governing board is held. At this meeting the pastor, the person chairing the meeting, the secretary, and perhaps the treasurer, may sit at a long table facing the other thirty-five members who are sitting in four or five or six rows of chairs facing the table. These chairs may be arranged in a fan-shaped, ninety-degree arc facing the table, but the focal point is the leadership team seated at the table. On the wall behind the table may be a large sheet of newsprint displaying the agenda for the meeting, perhaps a sheet of posterboard prepared by the treasurer as part of her monthly report, and possibly a screen on which will be projected a half dozen slides when a report is made to the board on the vacation Bible school held several months earlier. In this large-group meeting it is important there be a clearly defined physical focal point, while the small committee can meet around tables where the focal point diffuses among those present.

2. Although it overlaps the issue of seating arrangements, a second difference between small groups and large groups is the subject of eye contact. It is highly desirable to maximize the opportunity for eye contact among the participants of a small group. In a large group any effort to encourage eye contact among the participants will produce frustration. The larger the number of the participants in a large group, the greater the level of frustration when an effort is made to enhance eye contact among the members of that group. Therefore the larger the size of the group, the more irrelevant or diversionary is the issue of eye contact among the persons present.

3. In the small group it usually is not necessary to worry about the acoustics or to arrange the seating in a manner to maximize people's ability to hear one another.

In the large group the ability of all persons present to hear what is being said with a minimum of effort and without the distraction of competing sounds becomes a very important item in the functioning of that group. In general, the larger the number of people present, the more important is the subject of acoustics. For example, the congregation averaging twenty-five at worship can function acceptably despite the distraction of outside traffic noises or the siren at the firehouse next door or the crying of one or two babies. However, when that congregation, meeting in the same room, suddenly grows to an average attendance of one hundred, these same sounds become far more distracting, and the leaders feel compelled to do something about the noise level.

4. In the well-managed small group the internal communication system usually is informal, unstructured, and highly effective. In the large group the internal communication system must be intentional, systematized, structured, and redundant. It must

receive careful attention, or the deficiency in the quality of internal communication will reduce the cohesiveness and inhibit the effectiveness of the large group.

A common example of this is the adult Sunday school class with an average attendance of six to ten people. It can function very effectively without anyone making a special effort to manage the communication among the members. Everyone just naturally knows what is happening in the class and with the various members.

By contrast, the adult class with an average attendance of thirty-five or sixty or ninety members needs a telephone committee and/or a class newsletter and/or a regular column in the church newspaper and/or a period for announcements during each meeting of that class and/or a closely knit "grapevine" and/or a system for mailing informational notices to the members. The larger the class and/or the greater the turnover of membership in the class and/or the larger the congregation from which this class is drawn, the greater the need for a redundant internal communication system which uses three or four channels of communication.

5. When a small group of people come together for the first time, it often is very effective to take an hour or longer for introductions and to encourage each person to take five to fifteen minutes to share with the others his or her personal and religious pilgrimage. In a group of eight or nine this may require one or two hours, but it is worth it. This can be a very effective team-building procedure if the group is composed of strangers or acquaintances. It is a very effective technique for turning a collection of strangers into a cohesive group in a very brief period of time.

In a large group this same procedure will require two to twelve hours. The pressure of time will cause many participants to share only a very superficial autobiographical account. This causes some to feel cheated because they were more open than others. Others will be bored by the time required. Several will not be able to keep the stories and the faces connected in the proper relationship and eventually will be embarrassed by their error. Many will be frustrated by this diversion. They came in response to a call to a different agenda!

In a group of two dozen people who are together for the first time, the use of name-tags is as important as oral introductions. If the group is to be together for three or four or five days, it may be wise to use name-tags and delay the oral introductions until the second or third day when an hour may be set aside for sharing "who we are." The more relational, rather than functional, the agenda of the large group, the more willing the participants will be to allocate an hour to introductions. When the size of the group goes above forty participants, however, it usually will strain the capabilities of the participants to allocate more than twenty minutes of group time to introductions.[4] In general, the larger the group, the shorter the period of time that can be used for introductions.

(6.) In a small group it usually is effective and productive to build the agenda for that meeting by asking all of the members to share their concerns. These concerns constitute the heart of the agenda for that meeting of that group of people.

In a large group there may be too much heterogeneity among the members to build an agenda by informally soliciting the concerns of each one of the thirty or forty or ninety persons present. If this is attempted, and only a few respond, this means the agenda is the creation of a few and not of the group or of the persons who called the meeting. It may turn out that the newly created agenda has little overlap with the declared purpose of the meeting, and the result is that many leave feeling frustrated. Another possibility is that everyone makes a meaningful contribution to the agenda-building process, but too little time remains to completely cover that agenda. The result may be that many participants leave frustrated because their concerns were solicited and then ignored.

In general, the larger the group, the greater the expectation of the participants that those calling the meeting or the leaders will have prepared the agenda. The smaller the group, the more important it is for the participants to have a voice in building the agenda.

In parallel terms, the first item on the "business agenda" of the small group may be to consider the agenda for that meeting, to review, and perhaps to revise it. Usually it is a reinforcing tactic to encourage a small group to feel free to revise its agenda.

By contrast, however, any effort to revise the agenda usually will be a disruptive tactic with a large group unless the persons present have been meeting together regularly for several months or the group has been meeting more or less continuously for several hours in that session.

⑦ After a formal presentation to a small group, it usually is very helpful to solicit questions, responses, rebuttals, and comments from each of the members. In order to preserve the anonymity of the questioner a common technique is to encourage written questions. The person making the presentation responds to each of these written questions. Everyone leaves with his or her personal questions answered.

If this same technique is encouraged following a formal presentation to a large group, there is the risk that the people will take this literally. If each of sixty persons present writes out and turns in a question following a forty minute presentation, it may take two to three hours to respond to each of the sixty questions. This will bore a large proportion of those present. One alternative is to ignore all but what appear to be the six best quality or the six most relevant questions. This will alienate most of the remaining fifty-four who took the trouble to formulate and write out a question and then were ignored.

In general, the larger the size of the group, the shorter should be the time alloted for questions from the group.

⑧ The small group of six or seven participants is not as restricted by the clock and the calendar as is the large group.

A small group of five or six or seven people may agree to convene at 7:30 P.M. for a committee meeting. Two or three arrive a few minutes before the scheduled time and begin to socialize with one another. Gradually other members join them and suddenly one of them announces, "I guess we're all here; let's begin our meeting." Although they have been "meeting" for the past twenty minutes, the official meeting begins at 7:49 P.M., and probably no one feels frustrated over the nineteen-minute delay in getting started. If they do not complete their agenda, they usually find it reasonably easy to schedule another meeting within the next several days.

By contrast, if the large Board meeting scheduled for 7:30 P.M.

does not begin until 7:38 P.M., some of the forty-three persons present will feel "cheated" because they arrived on time and the group had to await the arrival of two or three irresponsible and thoughtless leaders who appear to be unaware of the time pressures on the rest of the members of the group. If they cannot complete their agenda and require a special meeting, it may be impossible to schedule it for at least two weeks, and then several of those present will miss it because of previous commitments.

In general, the larger the size of the group, the more important it becomes to begin meetings on time and to schedule meetings far in advance. Ignoring this generalization is one of the most effective means of increasing discontent and decreasing participation.

9. The small group can meet for a longer period of time before taking a break than can the large group.

A simple example of this is the lecture class of 600 college sophomores that meets for fifty minutes, but the graduate seminar can meet with that same professor for two hours or longer without a break.

The length of time people can meet without a break in the routine is one of the most important distinctions between large groups and small groups. The pastor can teach a Bible study class of a dozen adults for two hours without a break. If it is a discussion format with active participation by everyone in the class, they may go for three hours without taking a break. When that same pastor preaches to three hundred people on Sunday morning, it probably will be unwise for him to devote more than eighteen to twenty-five minutes to the sermon. If he is an exceptional orator, if the congregation stands for a hymn immediately before the sermon, and if they stand for another hymn immediately after the sermon, he may be able to hold the attention of the majority for much of the time during a twenty-five to thirty minute sermon.

In general, as the size of the group increases, the amount of time between breaks in the routine decreases. A committee meeting of seven people may run for three hours, but if the board, with thirty-six members, is to meet for more than two hours, there probably should be an official break after the first sixty to eighty minutes.

10. The basic and most important reward for attendance for members of the small group usually is in being together. The members of the small group enjoy being with one another. When the members of a continuing small group, such as an adult Sunday school class or a circle in the women's organization or a seven-member Christian education committee or a Bethel Series Bible study class go home, they usually look forward to the next gathering of that group of people. Simply being together is a strong motivating force in maintaining the regular attendance of the members whenever that small group gathers.

By contrast, more systematic attention must be given to rewarding attendance if a high proportion of the members is expected to be present for the regular meetings of large groups. The "automatic" attendance begins to decline when the group numbers more than three persons, it drops sharply when the size of the group exceeds seven persons, and the proportion of members who are present for a particular meeting continues to decline as the membership climbs past twenty. (The major exception to this generalization is when the large group is unified by several components of the "glue" described in item 11 on pages 36-37).

There are five common types of rewards for attendance that are widely used all across the North American continent.

The first is the personal visit or the postcard or the telephone call which appears to be a reminder of the time and place, but also conveys the message, "You are important. You are needed. We want to be sure you are present for our next meeting. We are willing to make this special effort to reward you in advance for planning to attend."

A second reward for attendance is the fulfillment of a loyalty commitment to a person (pastor, friend, chairperson of the committee, organizer of the group, and so on) or to a personal vow or to an organization by being present. When that individual goes home after the meeting, he or she feels rewarded for the time and energy expended by having fulfilled that personal loyalty commitment.

A third reward to the person attending a particular meeting or participating in a specific event can be summarized in the frequently heard response, "I'm glad I came! This was very meaningful and helpful to my personal and spiritual needs, and I leave feeling enriched and fulfilled." The reward is the personal or spiritual experience for the participant.

The fourth, and by far the most common, reward for attendance is food. When a twelve-member committee gathers, a very modest snack is sufficient. When an eighteen or twenty member council meeting or adult class is scheduled to meet, the refreshments should be, and often are, more elaborate. They may include a choice from among two or three beverages, plus one or two dessert-type items. If it is a very large group, however, the refreshments may be far more extensive. A simple illustration is the congregation where the adult Sunday school classes begin with a choice of coffee, orange juice, doughnuts, or rolls. When the nine-member Christian education committee meets, the members take turns providing a light snack. When the seventy-member administrative board gathers for its monthly meeting, however, they begin with socializing and dinner, gradually move on to dessert, and eventually get into the business agenda of the evening.

In general, the larger the size of the group and the greater the interest in encouraging a high proportion of the members to be present, the more important food becomes as a reward for attendance.

The fifth, and the least common, response to the need to systematically encourage attendance in large groups can be summarized by the word *satisfactions*. When the members go home from the meeting of a large group of people, they look forward to the next meeting of that group because of the satisfactions they derived from the meeting just ended.

In explaining why he never missed the monthly meeting of the eighty-four-member governing board at Trinity Church, a very busy man explained, "I enjoy these meetings! I always learn something. We have fun. And when it's over, I go home feeling that it was a worthwhile investment of my time because we got something done."

In more specific operational terms, the monthly board meetings at Trinity Church begin with a four or five minute devotional time led by one of the lay persons. This is followed by a fifteen-to-twenty-minute, carefully planned "learning period," during which the pastor leads a discussion on one lesson in churchmanship which lifts up a specific insight, concept, or question and relates it very precisely to what is happening at Trinity Church. The next fifty to ninety minutes are devoted to a carefully prepared agenda. This session is regularly interrupted by laughter and an occasional funny story. The pastor has intentionally nurtured an atmosphere that not only permits, but encourages, humor and laughter. The agenda is reproduced on a large sheet of newsprint, and as the evening proceeds, the chairperson uses a colored marker to cross off each item as it is disposed of by formal action. Just before the conclusion of the meeting the secretary takes thirty to forty seconds to summarize all that has been accomplished and to reinforce the feeling, "We've accomplished something tonight." This is followed by the benediction, refreshments, socializing, and a reinforcement of the feeling, "I'm glad I came."

By contrast, in a few congregations the monthly meeting of the governing board may dispose of a dozen items and issues in an efficient and satisfying manner during the first hours, then spend an hour or two bickering over a very complex or controversial or insoluble problem. As the board spends a long and frustrating period of time trying to nail that custard pie to the wall, one by one several members quietly slip away and finally the person chairing the meeting announces, "It's past the time we agreed on for adjournment, I'm not even sure we have a quorum left, and I don't believe we can settle this until we get more information. Let's stand. Reverend, will you dismiss us with the benediction?"

As the members who have stayed this long go home, the strongest memory they carry with them is the frustration generated by the discussion on the last item. Those who left earlier go home feeling guilty about leaving prematurely. Frustration and guilt are not healthy rewards for attendance.

11. In the well-managed small group, a large part of the cohesive and unifying force that holds that collection of individuals together is the close relationship of those individuals to one another. The group is the glue.

SMALL GROUPS AND LARGE GROUPS

In the well-managed large group, however, the relationships of the members with one another cannot be the sole or basic cohesive force or the large group will dissolve into cliques. Very, very few people can build close personal relationships with more than a dozen other persons—most of us have no more than seven or eight close personal friends.

The large group must either be (a) short-term or (b) reinforced with a series of other unifying and cohesive forces. These might include nationality; race; language; social class; kinship ties; a very strong allegiance to a magnetic leader; a strong loyalty to the parent organization; a specific, attainable, measurable, visible, unifying, and satisfying group goal; shared opposition to a common enemy; widely shared, deeply felt, and very precisely defined theological, philosophical, ideological, or political belief; a long history of growing old together; many years of meeting together in a familiar place; a common task that requires many people to accomplish it (the large sixty-eight-voice choir, for example); living together through a memorable crisis, such as a flood, a fire, or a tornado; or any of a variety of similar central organizing principles which bind a large collection of individuals into a unified and cohesive group.[5]

A simple example of the reinforing effect of these cohesive forces is the 380-member Swedish Lutheran Church (which is led by its forty-six-year-old pastor, who is in his sixteenth year there and also is the son of a former pastor) in its decision to relocate from an old neighborhood in the central city to a new suburban site. Fifteen years later, the relocation process is complete. The new building has been constructed. The mortgage has been retired. The pastor, after a twenty-five-year pastorate, moved and was followed by another minister who stayed three years. He was followed by the current pastor, who is of mixed German and Norwegian ancestry. The Swedish flavor of the congregation has disappeared. The members complain about the lack of a sense of direction, the loss of the feeling of unity, and the declining attendance patterns. Why? It is still a large group, but four of the basic unifying and cohesive forces (the nationality identity, the attachment to the old meeting place, the task of relocation to a new site, and the longtime pastor) have disappeared and have not been replaced.

The basic generalization is that the larger the number of persons in the group, the more important it becomes to reinforce the sense of unity with a series of cohesive forces such as those mentioned here. Frequently some elements of the glue begin to fade away and must be replaced with new glue. Thus a small group of five persons can meet for three hours on a serious agenda, no one cracks a joke, smiles, laughs, or displays any evidence of humor, and everyone can leave feeling very satisfied with what happened.

12. The large group rarely can meet for as long as two hours without the participants feeling the need for laughter, an occasional joke, and other expressions of levity. Humor and music are the essential lubricants in the management of the large group *unless the unity and cohesiveness is based on organizing against the enemy in which cases humor may be omitted,* but that is not necessarily healthy!

In general, the larger the size of the group and/or the more pronounced the absence of other cohesive and unifying forces (item 11 above) and/or the longer the period of time the people are together in that particular meeting and/or the larger the proportion of persons in the group who do not know the other persons present, the more important is the place of humor in the management of large groups.

13. Paralleling the place of humor is the changing role of music in managing the life of groups. In small groups music can be an asset, but for most small groups, music is a luxury, not an essential factor.

By contrast, music is an essential component in the management of most large groups. In the small congregation, for example, a choir is an asset, but it is not an essential element of a meaningful worship experience. The larger the congregation, the more significant is the quality of the chancel choir and the place of congregational singing.

A simple example of this is the relatively low priority given to music in the typical two-hundred-member congregation, but the very high priority given to the committee responsible for the music at the city-wide evangelistic services which it is expected will attract several thousand people. Among the most common illustrations of the importance of music in managing large groups of people are holiday street parades, the high school proms of the 1950s and 1970s, military organizations, the annual meeting of the denominational regional judicatory, and televised religious services.

14. The small group may be able to function very effectively for two to three hours at a stretch with a heavy emphasis on verbal communication and with little or no emphasis on visual communication.

The large group, however, rarely can function for more than ten consecutive minutes *as a group* if the total emphasis is on one-way verbal communication. This emphasis on verbal communication must be interrupted periodically by music, applause, tears, standing and sitting, visual communication, recesses, offerings, group singing, laughter, or other nonverbal forms of communication and expression. If this is not done, the large group begins to disintegrate into a collection of cliques, ad hoc small groups, subcommittees, and disenchanted individuals.

Perhaps one of the most obvious examples of this is the motion picture which can hold an audience's attention for two hours or longer, but the stage play (with its heavier emphasis on verbal communication) usually is divided into two or three or four acts with an intermission between acts.

Less obvious, but equally significant, is the difference between the typical Black preacher, who often can hold the attention of a large congregation for a sermon lasting an hour or longer, while very few white preachers can hold the attention of the audience for longer than twenty minutes. Why? One of the major reasons is that Black preachers tend to draw more word pictures in their sermons and to use unambiguous words which clearly communicate a meaning that can be visualized very easily. By contrast, white preachers tend to present abstract concepts and to choose ambiguous words which must be defined by the context in which they are used (see chapter 5 for an elaboration of this distinction between visual and verbal).

15. The small group can function very effectively for a long period of time without a project or task or any reference to the needs of people outside that group. It may become exclusionary and/or

ingrown, but it can continue to meet the needs of the members.

The large group, however, has great difficulty functioning for any substantial period of time if the focus is completely on the members of that group. Sooner or later it will begin to (a) focus on the needs of non-members or (b) become militantly exclusionary or (c) break up into cliques and factions or (d) disintegrate as a large group.

This distinction is of tremendous significance in (a) planning strategies for congregations of different sizes and (b) defining the purpose and role of such auxiliary organizations as the church school, the women's organization, the youth fellowship, and the men's brotherhood.

From a denominational perspective the recommended program or congregational emphasis in a particular year should reflect differences in the size of the churches, as well as a definition of the nature and purpose of the worshiping congregation. To develop and attempt to propagate a program or strategy that will be relevant to the small single-cell church[6] and to the larger and more complex four-hundred-member congregation is to engage in an exercise designed to produce frustration, guilt, and low morale.

From a congregational perspective if the programmatic structure for the auxiliary organization is to focus on the creation of small (seven to fifteen persons) face-to-face subgroups, it is logical and, perhaps even wise, to eliminate projects, treasurers, special bank accounts, bazaars, Sunday school picnics, Rally Days, contests, and any major emphasis on an evangelistic outreach.

If, however, the emphases in these auxiliary organizations include (a) developing a sense of loyalty to the auxiliary organization itself (Sunday school, women's organization, men's brotherhood, youth fellowship, etc.) as well as to the subgroups in the auxiliary, (b) an intentional and systematic evangelistic outreach to people outside any worshiping congregation, (c) inviting and assimilating of new people into that organization, (d) nurturing and rewarding nonverbal creative skills and/or (e) encouraging the members of these auxiliary organizations to see themselves as responsible members of God's Universal Church (as well as members of a specific congregation), this distinction between small groups and large groups becomes very important.

In general, it suggests that any large group, such as the participants in the church school, or any middle-sized group, such as the twenty-five ladies who are active members of the women's organization, or the forty-member youth group, requires a means of expressing its interest in and concern for people outside that collection of individuals *if it is to function as a healthy, vital, and open large group on a continuing basis.* This expression of concern for others may be in the form of calling on shut-ins or the financial support of a mission project or of serving as a conduit between a source of volunteers and the inner city school that needs a corps of unpaid tutors for one-to-one teaching or a work camp experience for teen-agers or a bazaar to raise money for responding to the emergencies of the needy or serving as foster grandparents in the church-sponsored nursery school or providing scholarships for seminarians. The details of "the project" are less important in this discussion than is the critical value of large groups having a means of organizing and expressing their corporate concern for others.

In simple terms, large groups need an organized means of expressing the collective concern of the members for non-members. This is not a basic need of small groups. The expression of this concern through a collective task or project is one of the forms of the "glue" (see item 11 above) that helps to hold the members of a large group together.

A fairly common institutional expression of the impact of ignoring this generalization can be seen in scores of congregations which (a) have placed a high priority on nurturing small groups in the church and (b) have barred bazaars, projects, separate bank accounts, or treasuries for the auxiliary organizations in order to promote a unified budget and special offerings. These two policies in regard to the group life of the congregation often undermine the strength of the auxiliary organizations and produce a plateau or decline in the membership growth curve of both the auxiliary organizations and the congregation.

16. One of the most important, but also one of the most widely neglected, distinctions between the internal dynamics of small

groups and the behavior patterns of large groups is the expectations by the group of the leader or leaders.

Although the research on small groups indicates that the competence of the leader is very important, in the typical small group the designated leader can, and often should act as a facilitator. The success or failure of a particular group experience or event depends very heavily on how effectively the members carry out their responsibilities to the other members of that small group. The primary role of the leader of the small group is to enable the members to exercise their gifts and talents.

In the large group a far greater responsibility rests on the leadership. The persons who are designated as the leaders of large groups may respond to this in very different ways. Those who feel most comfortable in working with small groups often will divide the large group into a series of small groups and continue the appropriate small group methodology with each group. Others will divide the large group into small groups at various times, attempt to develop the interaction among the people within the several small groups and also within the occasional plenary session. A few will be able to help the large group function as one large group by reinforcing the basic organizing principles (point 11 above), by the seating arrangements, by regular breaks in the routine, by carefully monitoring the anxiety level to insure a good learning experience, by repeatedly lifting up the basic focal point of the gathering, and by other techniques in the management of large groups. A highly skilled manager of large groups can cause 5,000 tired people to sit through three-hour plenary sessions every evening for five consecutive evenings and go to bed every night delighted they were there and determined to return the following night.

In reviewing these contrasting responses of various group leaders, the basic point for this discussion is that each leader usually responds on the basis of his or her own competence, value system, and priorities, *not on the basis of the expectations of the members of the group*. The person who is highly skilled and comfortable in working with small groups, but who has little or no experience in working with large or very large groups naturally will encourage dividing a large assemblage of people into small groups. Every leader naturally attempts to remold a situation into the structure or agenda with which that leader is most comfortable! That is normal human behavior.

The sensitive (which is not always a synonym for skilled or experienced) group leader will be aware that the large group normally has a different set of expectations of the leader than those held by the typical small group and will attempt to adjust his or her leadership style to be responsive to the needs of different size groups. *This is a radically different response than attempting to adjust the size of the group to fit the competence style of the leader!*

Although there are many individual exceptions, in general, the larger the size of the group the more likely the participants will expect the leader(s) to (a) define the agenda, (b) set the schedule, (c) adhere very closely to the announced agenda and schedule, (d) determine the pace at which the group will move, (e) adjust the schedule or agenda in response to the changing mood of the group, (f) exercise a strong initiating leadership role, (g) care for minor details in regard to the meeting and functioning of the group "without bothering the participants" with these details, (h) manage any conflict that may emerge among the members of the group, (i) display a comparatively high level of competence at anticipating and planning for the immediate future, (j) demonstrate the ability to function in a strong leadership role when the situation suddenly requires a strong leader, (k) exhibit a contagious sense of humor, (l) possess an above-average level of competence in verbal skills, and last, but far from least important, (m) adjourn the meeting on, or slightly ahead of, schedule!

A simple operational illustration of this list is that it often describes the changing expectations placed on the minister who moves from the ninety-year-old, 135-member congregation to become the pastor of the twenty-seven-year-old, 960-member congregation. It also may describe the changing expectations on the lay person who has been teaching a class of five young married couples and then accepted the responsibility of teaching a class of forty to fifty mature adults.

In general, the larger and/or the less cohesive the group, the greater the expectations the members have for the leader(s) to exercise a strong, initiating, and directive leadership style.

17. A closely related factor is that the workload of the leader varies with (a) the size of the groups in an organization and (b) the leadership style of the leader.

This distinction between the implications of an emphasis on small groups and emphasis on large groups can be illustrated by looking at the leadership style and workload of pastors. Many ministers specialize in doing things themselves, while a comparatively small number specialize in getting things done by others rather than actually doing it themselves.

The minister who specializes in doing things and who places a high priority on organizing and working with small groups rarely is able to be an effective pastor, except perhaps as part of a multiple staff, in a congregation with more than 200 members. When that combination of leadership style and emphasis on small groups is found in a pastor serving a congregation with several hundred members, the end product usually includes an overworked and frustrated minister, a neglected pastor's family, a large proportion of relatively inactive members, many of whom feel neglected and ignored, a strong affirmation of that minister by the more active members of the fifteen-to-twenty small groups, a leveling off or decline in the membership growth curve, comparatively poor assimilation of new members, an imbalance in the total program of that church, gradually mounting discontent with the pastor, and, eventually, an effort to encourage the pastor to resign.

By contrast, the pastor who has developed a high level of competence in causing things to happen, rather than in doing all the work by himself or herself, and who also specializes in building the life of a congregation around small groups, can be an effective pastor in the congregation with 300 or 500 members without feeling overworked. (It should be noted here that close to 60 percent of all Protestant congregations on the North American continent have fewer than 250 members, slightly over 20 percent include between 250 and 500 members, approximately 10 percent report between 500 and 750 members, and only one Protestant congregation in ten has more than 750 resident members.)

SMALL GROUPS AND LARGE GROUPS

The one Protestant congregation in five with more than 500 resident members requires either (a) a pastor who has at least a moderate level of competence in nurturing large groups and who specializes in causing things to happen rather than doing everything unilaterally or (b) one full-time program staff person for each 200 members or (c) a widespread acceptance of a relatively low level of involvement and participation by a large proportion of the members in the ongoing life, ministry, program, and outreach of that congregation. Rather than recognizing and acting on the distinctive differences between the internal dynamics of small groups and the behavior patterns of large groups, the common approach is to identify a pastor who has been very effective in working with small groups in a congregation of 150 to 300 members, to ask that minister to move to a much larger congregation which needs a minister with competence in managing large groups, and to wonder why that minister now complains about being overworked and frustrated. After all, a really committed Christian minister should be grateful for that "promotion," rather than unhappy about the workload!

18. One of the reasons for the leadership problems identified here is the result of another distinction between small groups and large groups.

The skills required for the effective management of small groups can be communicated from one person to another very easily. Many individuals can become very adept at the management of small groups in a brief period of time. It appears that many individuals have a natural or intuitive gift or talent in facilitating the functioning of small groups.

The varieties of gifts and competencies required for the effective management of large groups, however, are far more difficult to identify, to communicate, and to learn. Relatively few people find it easy to master these skills, and they do not appear to be consistent with the intuitive responses of most people.

19. Another basic distinction between small or middle-size groups and large groups which has significant implications for leadership is the place of competition. Competition between groups can be destructive to the morale and sense of unity of the

45

members of the small or middle-size groups, but large groups usually are strengthened by competition. Frequently, in fact, very large groups thrive on competition.

Thus, for example, the Sunday school organized with very large adult classes of seventy or eighty or one hundred persons often will encourage competition among the classes for attendance (the banner class), for recruiting new members, for the mission giving, and for the size and impressiveness of class projects. By contrast, the Sunday school organized around small groups will be well advised to avoid interclass competition.

During the first four decades of this century most high schools were designed to serve the residents of a relatively small geographical area, and many high schools had fewer than thirty or forty students in each grade. The interscholastic athletic programs in these small rural high schools emphasized participation. Following the wave of school consolidations of the 1940s and 1950s, the emphasis on interscholastic athletic programs shifted from participation to winning. The larger schools could afford the costs and needed the benefits of highly competitive sports.

Likewise small businesses with ten or twenty or thirty employees usually emphasize customer service while the management of the huge corporation concentrates on increasing its share of the market.

The pastors of the large churches frequently refer to their "competitors," but the pastors of small congregations usually concentrate on either the quality of congregational life or intercongregational cooperation.

20. Another significant distinction between groups of different sizes that has implications for leaders is the ability of long-established small groups to continue to function effectively despite a break in the continuity of the leadership. By contrast, the large group frequently begins to deteriorate when there is a break in the continuity of leadership. This generalization can be illustrated by two very common examples.

The small, tightly knit, rural congregation averaging thirty-five or forty at worship may be served by a part-time preacher who leaves after two or three years. After several months with different visiting preachers, a new "permanent" part-time minister is found who stays for another two years, and then the pulpit is vacant again for several months before a replacement is found. During all these years the worship attendance rarely drops below thirty-five or climbs above forty.

After nine years the pastor of the 600-member congregation resigns, and that pulpit is filled by a series of visiting preachers for several months until the successor arrives. Typically the worship attendance—and the financial support—decline during the period the congregation is without a pastor, and it may take several months following the arrival of the new minister before the worship attendance is back up to the earlier level.

The Men's Bible Class taught by Dr. Roberts has had a Sunday morning attendance ranging between seventy and eighty ever since he began teaching it eleven years ago. Two years after he retired and moved to Florida, the attendance was down to thirty-five and now, a decade later, it rarely exceeds one dozen.

The Lydian Class was formed in 1943 by a group of business and professional women. Today all but two are retired, the class is down to an average attendance of ten to twelve, and it is a remarkably redemptive, loving, caring, and supportive group of women born in the first decade of this century. It matters very little who is assigned to teach this class, although they prefer the same teacher for at least three or four consecutive Sundays. Attendance always runs between ten and twelve.

In general, the larger the group, the more vulnerable it is to institutional deterioration when there is a change in the leadership. This is one reason why it is rare to find large and rapidly growing congregations, *that have sustained that growth*, with a succession of short pastorates. (One of the most effective methods of discouraging the numerical growth of a denomination is to encourage short pastorates in the large congregations of that denominational family.)

21. The capability of a group to assimilate new members also is related to its size, as well as to other factors.

Laboratory experiments, for example, reveal that a group of four strangers, coming together for the first time, usually find it comparatively easy to absorb three new members, but when the group reaches seven members, potential new members encounter resistance. By contrast, the large group of twenty-two persons can absorb a half dozen newcomers without difficulty.

When major corporations began to feel the pressure in the mid-1970s to increase the number of outside directors, it was found that the companies with fewer than eleven directors could add two or three new directors very easily, but the companies with fourteen or fifteen directors usually faced the uncomfortable task of removing some outside directors in order to make room for the new outside directors without becoming a large group.[7]

In general, the very small group changes significantly when its membership goes above seven or eight while the larger small group tends to resist growing beyond fifteen or sixteen or seventeen members. Thus growth is not simply a function of adding new members; it also is a function of the size of the group. In addition, most groups, regardless of size, find that the distinctive quality of the group changes when net growth approaches the point that it results in a doubling in the size of that collection of people. A very common cost of doubling in size is that some of the original members drop out. It no longer is the same group as the one to which they had made an earlier commitment, so they find it easier to drop out than to remain active.

The one major exception to this set of generalizations is the group which has a specific, attainable, measurable, visible, satisfying, and unifying goal which requires more hands to accomplish that task. Thus the congregation engaged in building its own meeting place with volunteer help can triple in size and also assimilate all the new members that are a part of this rapid growth. The eleven-member Men's Brotherhood, which is involved in attempting to raise $3,600 for missions by serving a community dinner six times a year, also can triple in size and assimilate all the new members who come in to help on this project. The four ladies, all in their seventies, who gather to sew every Tuesday, can absorb four or five additional members, if each one is a good seamstress.

22. Related to the size, stability, and growth potential of groups is the issue of group maintenance. In general, the larger the group,

the more extensive the need to systematically and intentionally maintain a sense of unity, cohesiveness, and common purpose.

This issue often floats to the top of the agenda whenever a group of more than seven or eight or nine persons changes the primary purpose for the existence of that group.[8] If and when the basic reason for the group's existence has been achieved, the more likely the need for the leaders to be concerned above group maintenance.

The nature of the group maintenance need changes, however, as the size of the group rises above a score or more of members. For example, the cohesive forces (item 11) which characterize the small group of five to fifteen people, often are very different from the critical cohesive and unifying forces in a group of seventy or two hundred. Therefore the focus of the group maintenance will change as the size of the group increases. Name-tags, for example, are superfluous in a long-established and stable congregation of thirty members, but they are a very useful group maintenance tool in the growing congregation of six hundred members.

23. The internal pressures on the members to respond to group goals are comparatively strong in small groups and diminish as the group increases in size.

Several years ago, in one of the leading books on small groups, a pioneer in the field pointed out that the smaller the group, the greater the "natural" motivation; the smaller the group, the less clearly defined is the assignment or the task, but this is no barrier to participation; the larger the group, the less internal pressure to participate; the larger the group, the easier for a few to control the direction of the group; the larger the group, the more difficult it is to find volunteers; and the larger the group, the more difficult for each member to express individual feelings.[9]

In other words, depersonalization increases as the size of the group rises, although a basic reason for creating small groups is to affirm the distinctive identity of each person.

This list of twenty-three factors which distinguish the internal dynamics of small groups from large groups is offered, not as an exhaustive and complete catalog, but rather to illustrate why it is of basic importance in church planning to recognize this distinction and why many small-group techniques may be counterproductive

EFFECTIVE CHURCH PLANNING

when used with large groups. Discussions of these differences often result in the raising of three other questions that merit attention here.

Is Bigger Better?

The first of these three issues is the natural product of communication difficulties. Discussions such as this one often operate on three levels. The first—and the level on which this discussion has been carried on—is simply descriptive. This is how it is. A second, and more complex level revolves around the question "Why is it that way?" This is usually a more interesting, but also more speculative level of discussion. The third, and the most abstract level revolves around the question "Is that good?" This is the level at which the discussion rests on value systems. Almost certainly many of the readers were at this level at several points in this chapter. One of the value questions raised here concerns the concept of "managing" the group life of the congregation. That issue is discussed in the next section of this chapter.

Another value question that arises in this type of discussion is "Are large groups better than small groups, or are small groups better than large groups?" Thus far the effort has been made to avoid that question. The only value judgment implicit in the discussion to this point is that it is counterproductive to assume there is no difference between large groups and small groups or to use small group techniques in managing large groups.

Within the churches, however, there is a widespread operational assumption that bigger is better. This can be seen in the encouragement given to the merger of small congregations, the status or prestige assigned to large churches, the "promotion" patterns in the careers of ministers, the widespread pattern of selecting denominational lay leadership from the larger congregations, and in dozens of other ways. This bigger is better value also is reflected in the frequently articulated "wish" by members of the small group of seven to twelve members (such as the youth fellowship, an adult Sunday school class, a circle in the women's organization, a prayer group, and others) that "I wish we could attract more members." In recent years, however, an impressive amount of research has been accumulating that suggests that in person-centered organizations, smaller may be better. The final paragraph of one pioneering study responds to the question, "What size should a school be?" The author concludes, "The data of this research and our own educational values tell us that a school should be sufficiently small that all of its students are needed for its enterprises. A school should be small enough that students are not redundant."[10] A more recent review of the many studies of American high schools reported that a recurring theme from these studies is that high schools should be limited to an enrollment of 500 or less.[11]

When the focus is shifted from schools to churches, a similar pattern can be seen. If a high value is placed on meaningful participation, the proportion of members attending corporate worship, the spontaneity of the caring and supportive fellowship among the members, the personal and spiritual growth of the members, the quality of the relationship between the pastor and the members, the opportunity for people to express their commitment to Jesus Christ as Lord and Savior through the worshiping congregation, the nurturing of the creative skills of the members, and the sense of being a called-out community, a strong case can be made for the thesis that the maximum size of a congregation should be 150 to 200 members (60 to 90 households) with a full-time pastor who has a high level of competence in developing and nurturing small groups. There are hundreds of congregations of this size which average 120 to 200 at corporate worship, are completely financially self-supporting, have a tremendous system of congregational care, provide a variety of opportunities for the personal and spiritual growth of the members, offer a challenging vocation to the pastor, and display a strong missional thrust to people and causes beyond the membership.

In the real world, however, there is still a premium on bigness and perhaps one-half or more of all full-time pastors are serving congregations with more than 300 members. This means that it is very important for at least one-half of all pastors to recognize the differences between the internal dynamics of small groups and the behavior patterns of large groups and to develop skills in working with large groups of people.

Alternatives to Management

Although it may be a diversionary question, a significant proportion of the clergy and a tiny fraction of the laity object to the value system expressed in the concept of the management of the group life of the worshiping congregation. Apparently they feel that in a Christian community no one should attempt to manage other people. That is not Christian! People should be free to be themselves and not be managed by others!

This is a totally unrealistic concept in any congregation which averages thirty or more at corporate worship! The congregation with forty or two hundred or five hundred members must be managed. Someone has to set the meeting time and place for corporate worship, select a pianist or an organist if musical instruments are to be used, provide seats or pews for the worshipers, select the hymns, schedule the rehearsal for the choir, assign the rooms to be used by the Sunday school classes, select the place and the date for the meeting of the governing board, decide if the minister is to receive any financial compensation and the amount if the minister is to be paid, select the congregational leaders, determine the size of the various study and prayer groups, arrange to heat the meeting place in cold weather, and decide whether offstreet parking shall be provided or not. Each one of these, and scores of other managerial questions, must be decided by someone. In each one the decision can be made in terms of enhancing the small group life of that congregation *or* in terms of enriching the large group life of that congregation. Rarely can a decision on these and similar questions be made without affecting the group life of that congregation.

There are four basic alternatives open to the pastor when it comes to the management of the group life of the parish. There is no neutral approach to this question. Just as there is no neutral or objective or unbiased approach to planning (see chapter 3), there is no neutral approach to the management of the group life of the parish.

Therefore, the first alternative open to the pastor (or the lay leader) is to manage the group life in a manner that is consistent with the value system and goals of that pastor. This may produce some conflicts when the values and goals of the pastor are not the same as the values and goals of the congregation—and of course, these are not the same for each member. How this conflict will be solved will be influenced by the value system and the goals of the pastor. If the pastor is unwilling to recognize that every person has a value system and a set of goals, that is ignorance. If the pastor is unwilling to manage the group life of the congregation in a manner that is consistent with that pastor's value system and goals, that means looking at other alternatives. One is an abdication of leadership by the pastor.

In other words, a second alternative in the management of group life of the parish is for the pastor to default on his or her responsibilities as the professional leader of the congregation and to encourage or allow one or more individuals in the congregation to manage the group life in accordance with their values and goals.

A common example of this is to pick an individual to lead the women's organization and to give her control over the management of the subgroups of that organization. A not uncommon result has been for this new president to (a) reduce the number of subgroups, (b) consolidate two or three of the smallest groups into one (hopefully) large group, (c) require the members to move to a new group every year in order to make new friends, (d) expect each subgroup to follow the same basic format at the monthly meetings, (e) eliminate all projects, bazaars, and dinners which reward nonverbal skills and creativity, (f) change the name of the organization, (g) encourage the subgroups to meet during the day, and (h) expect all subgroups to make a study of the same topic the major theme of the monthly meeting. These represent tried-and-true methods of turning a large organization into a small organization! A parallel pattern often can be seen when one person dominates the Sunday school, the men's organization, the creation of a series of Bible study groups, the youth ministries, or the music program. In each case there may be an unintentional "cutback" dimension built into the default by the pastor of a professional leadership role in the management of the group life of that congregation. (The broad generalization that covers this point is that the vast majority of lay-controlled congregations tend to be small in size and/or declining in numbers. In nearly all large and rapidly growing congregations the decision-making processes are heavily influenced by the pastor. The normal and natural tendency of the laity is to act in a manner that encourages the development of a small, intimate, loving, caring, and redemptive fellowship where every member knows every other member and where is is easy for every person to know everything that is happening.)

A third alternative open to the pastor, when it comes to the management of the group life of the congregation, is to attempt to avoid the whole subject by emphasizing, "We are one big happy family, and we should try to do everything as a congregation rather than break up into groups and cliques." This is a widely followed approach to this issue. The easiest means of achieving this goal of conceptualizing the congregation as one large group, rather than as a congregation of groups and individuals, is to limit the size to less than forty active and participating members, to emphasize a homogeneous (rather than pluralistic) membership, and to divide the total membership into two categories: "those of us who carry the load and do the work around here" and "those who do not take their membership vows seriously."

A far less common, but similar variation of this alternative is to develop a large (sometimes huge) congregation which functions as one large group of several hundred members rather than as a congregation of many subgroups, plus those individuals who do not see themselves as a part of any group. This is very difficult to accomplish, but when it does occur, the resulting congregation usually includes several of these characteristics: (a) a remarkably high degree of homogeneity among the members, (b) several very strong and cohesive unifying forces (see item 11 above) such as nationality or language or being organized against a common enemy or a widely shared distinctive theological stance, (c) very strong and unifying pastoral leadership, (d) very few second generation members, (e) a strong identification with a meeting place, (f) widely supported and highly visible unifying congregational goals (such as building a new meeting place or a television program or organizing and operating a private school or college), and, most important of all, (g) a leader, usually the pastor, with exceptional gifts and talents in the management of very large groups of people.

In addition to these first three alternatives to managing the group life of the congregation of (a) doing it unilaterally or (b) abdicating responsibility or (c) ignoring it and functioning as one large group, there is a fourth alternative open to nearly every pastor. This is to distinguish between the means to an end and the purpose of the worshiping congregation, to see the management of the group life of that congregation as a means to an end rather than as an end in itself, to work with the members in identifying the values and goals that congregation is seeking to promote and achieve, to facilitate setting priorities among those values and goals, and to develop a broad consensus for that system of values, goals, and priorities. That mosaic of decision then can be used as the context for making the decisions which are involved in managing the group life of that congregation.

In very simple terms the question is not, do you favor someone managing the group life of your congregation? The real questions are (1) Who will do it? and (2) What will be the values, goals, and priorities that determine how the group life will be managed?

Cliques or Members?

One of the most important products of the management of the group life of a congregation is reflected in the degree to which members of groups feel a sense of belonging to that congregation as a whole. Before going on to suggest a positive response to one of the most neglected factors in managing the group life of a congregation, it may be helpful to identify some of the more common symptoms of the problem. One set of symptoms may be encountered in those congregations in which there is a strong and intentional effort to encourage the organization of formal groups, both small and large, and where membership in these groups is very meaningful to most of the members. Some of these may be primarily task-oriented groups, while others are primarily relational groups.

Eventually, to use one example, after the investment of a considerable effort, there emerged several tightly knit and cohesive groups in that particular congregation of six hundred members. These included a thirty-five voice adult choir; four adult Sunday school classes; a young single adult group which meets once a month with an attendance ranging from sixty to over two hundred, a mutual support group composed of twenty-five widowed persons; a high school youth choir with twenty-eight regular participants; a Tuesday evening discussion group composed of eighteen to twenty recently divorced younger women; a Friday afternoon sewing group of seven women in their late sixties and seventies; a men's Bible study and prayer group that meets for an hour at 6:30 A.M. every Monday; a Thursday afternoon women's Bible study group with an average attendance of seven or eight, a group of thirty-five volunteers who spend an average of two hours a week tutoring at an inner city school; a Wednesday morning prayer circle of nine women; a group of two dozen formerly married adults in their forties and early fifties who meet as a study group on Wednesday evening, as a social group on Friday nights, and as an adult class on Sunday morning, a book review circle of a dozen women that meets once a month, a young parents' class that meets as a study group on two Monday evenings every month and goes bowling the other two Monday evenings, a group of developmentally disabled persons and their parents who meet at the church every Tuesday evening, and a variety of other groups and organizations which frequently are a part of the organizational life of a congregation of that size. Overall it is a very impressive picture in terms of ministry, outreach, a response to the needs of people, expressions of Christian concern, and program development.

In talking with the longtime members of that congregation,

three types of comments were heard repeatedly. "It's true we have a lot of new programs, but have you noticed how few of our own members are involved?" "I don't have any objections to all of these new programs, but I am concerned over how few of those people are coming forward to join our church." "This may impress you, but to me it's just that many more little cliques where the people are concerned only for themselves and don't care a bit about the rest of us or about this church."

In this example many people have a strong sense of belonging to a particular group, but apparently most of them are not formal members of the congregation which is the umbrella organization for all these groups. A second example of the same basic pattern illustrates how people may be formal members of a congregation, but not all of them feel the same sense of belonging or identification with that local church and lifts up another set of symptoms.

"The easiest way for you to understand my role here," explained the 33-year-old minister of the eighty-seven-year-old Oak Grove Church, "is to recognize that I am really the pastor of two congregations. For more than seventy years this was a stable, small rural congregation with fewer than two hundred members. About seven years ago several developers started building houses out here, and within a few years we doubled in size. But we're not really one congregation, we're two. One congregation is made up of the old-timers who've been here for decades. The other congregation is made up of the newcomers who never have been fully accepted out here.

"Actually," he reflected after a slight pause, "I guess I really should describe this as four congregations. The first is made up of the old-timers I mentioned a moment ago. The second is an adult Sunday school class that was started about five years ago. It is composed of two dozen people from that first wave of new families who moved out here, and it is a very close-knit and cohesive group. Most of them are in their late thirties or early forties. They have their own officers, their own monthly social events, their own treasury, and, in many ways, act like a small congregation all by themselves. The third is a group that started out when several young mothers got together on their own and began to meet every

Monday morning in one of their homes. About a year ago they changed to an evening meeting time in order to include the husbands. Now they meet on a regular basis on the first Tuesday of every month, plus every once in a while for a party or picnic or some other kind of outing. There are about fifteen couples in the group, they range in age from 26 to 35 and every one of them joined this congregation since I came here three years ago. The fourth congregation is composed of the other eighty-five or ninety people who have joined since the first subdivision opened here about seven years ago. If we keep on growing at this rate, we're going to have to move to a new site and build a new building."

Six years later a visit to the same pastor of that same congregation elicited this observation as he proudly showed his visitor around the 26-month-old, $350,000 building on a new seven-acre site out on the edge of town. "When you were here before, I told you we would have to relocate if we kept on growing. Well, the Sunday we moved in here, we had 583 members on the roll, and I expect we will pass the 700 mark by the end of this year. Funny thing though, I still feel that I'm the pastor of two congregations, those who joined before we relocated and those who have come in since we moved here. Although it was a headache in many ways, moving to a new site and building a new church sure united the people who were in on that process. We didn't have enough money to hire all of the work done, and we had to rely on a lot of volunteers. The general contractor says we have $50,000 worth of volunteer labor in this place—and over half of that came from the people who joined since I came here nine years ago."

If one shifts the focus from the details to the larger picture, this pastor was describing two very common phenomena in the group life of a rapidly growing congregation.

In both conversations he was referring to "closure," or the tendency of a group of people to exclude potential new members of that group. The old-timers cause the newcomers to feel like intruders or trespassers. Nearly every continuing group of people, either large or small, goes through some shared experiences which tend to bind together those who have shared that experience. They feel a sense of cohesiveness and tend to create unintentional and invisible walls which cause newcomers, who have not shared in that common experience, to feel like outsiders. A group of four strangers, for example, may come together and begin to work on an assigned task. Ten minutes later a person who comes along and attempts to join that group will experience a strong feeling of being unneeded, unwanted, and unwelcome. Closure does not always take years! It may happen within minutes after a group is formed! In the example described here, a major point of closure occurred when the need for lay volunteer construction help ended and with the completion of the new building.

The second phenomenon can be described in anthropological terms as the process by which new members are welcomed or "initiated into the tribe." Every tribe, congregation, group, nation, family, voluntary association, class, organization, sorority, fraternity, or service club has a formal or informal procedure for initiating new members into that tribe. In many Christian congregations the formalized initiatory rites include baptism and/or confirmation and/or transfer of a letter of membership from another congregation and/or participation in a membership training class and/or examination by officials of that congregation.

In addition to these formal rites of passage or initiatory ceremonies, there is another set of events that are of fundamental importance in managing the group life of a congregation and in preventing unnecessary problems. The basic symptoms of this problem were illustrated by the two case studies presented earlier. In the first example, people became members of very meaningful groups, but most of them apparently never gained any feeling of "belonging" to the sponsoring congregation and did not develop a sense of loyalty to that local church. This was emphasized repeatedly by many of the longtime members who apparently believed either (a) that people joining these new groups should become loyal members of that congregation or (b) these new programs and groups should have a stronger orientation toward serving the existing membership.

In the second example, newcomers to the community were received as members, apparently largely on the initiative of the pastor, but many of these new members had difficulty gaining a sense of acceptance into this long-established, but now rapidly growing, congregation.

Both congregations were deficient in their capability to initiate people into that tribe. This is a widespread problem, and it is magnified by the common illusion that when a person is formally received into membership in the congregation or becomes a member of a small subgroup, that automatically produces a sense of acceptance and a feeling of belonging to that congregation.

If one looks beyond the formal initiatory rites, there are three widely used routes by which newcomers are welcomed into a congregation. One of these is appropriate for those congregations, such as the first example described earlier, where people join the groups organized by a local church, but relatively few of them develop any sense of belonging to that congregation. In many churches a conscious and intentional effort is made to initiate the members of these groups into the tribe by asking the group to accept responsibility for implementing a specific and highly visible congregational goal which has a clearly defined terminal date. In one church the young single adult group has the total responsibility for the annual all-church picnic. In another congregation an adult Sunday school class of young married couples was asked to produce a picture directory of the membership as a class project. Other examples include asking one group to prepare a huge wall banner depicting the major events in the seventy-year history of that congregation, enlisting another group to take the responsibility for the 3 P.M., December 24 "Birthday Party for Jesus" for young children and their parents, recruiting another group to plan the annual celebration of the anniversary of the founding of that congregation, finding another group willing to plan the annual Thanksgiving worship service and dinner at church, and securing a group to take the responsibility for repainting the fellowship hall.

In each case a group that saw itself on the periphery of the larger fellowship circle gained a sense of belonging by implementing a congregation-wide goal. In each case the project was a unifying experience for the members of that subgroup, and especially for the newest members. In each case the group gained a measure of appreciation from the congregation for its highly visible contribution. In each case the definition of a terminal date made it easier for the group to accept that responsibility. In each case the implementation of this congregation-wide goal caused the members of the subgroup to become better acquainted with members of that congregation who previously had been strangers. In each case the lontime members acquired a new awareness of and appreciation for a particular subgroup with which they were comparatively unacquainted. In each case the task was a significant initiatory rite for the members of that subgroup.

A second and more widely used method of initiating people on the periphery of congregational life into the fellowship circle is to focus, not on the group as a whole, but on individuals. In one small town congregation the twenty-four-year-old son of a leading family brought back a bride from a far-off country. Subsequently, she was received into membership in that congregation, but she was initiated into the tribe when on a Tuesday several months later she arrived in the church kitchen at nine in the morning to help prepare the big annual church-sponsored turkey dinner. When she went home, bone tired, at ten that evening, she left behind a circle of close friends, most of whom had been acquaintances or strangers that morning.

In a large central city church new members are received at the 11 A.M. worship service on the second Sunday of every month. After a brief reception following conclusion of the worship service, they meet with the part-time minister of visitation for lunch, for a quick review of what they learned about that congregation in their membership classes, and for a forty-minute training session in making visitation-evangelism calls. At two o'clock they go out in pairs to call on prospective members who have been identified by the minister of evangelism. When they return at four, for refreshments and to share their experiences, these new members have been initiated into the tribe! After calling for two hours on behalf of that congregation, they feel a sense of identity with the congregation.

Other congregations have policies which expect each new member to accept a specific responsibility such as helping to teach Sunday school, serving as part of a visitation team that calls on neglected people in the county nursing home, passing out the permanent name-tags early Sunday morning and collecting them after the 11 o'clock worship service, serving as a deacon or as an usher, working in the vacation Bible school, becoming part of the crew which meets one Saturday a month for general maintenance work at the church, joining a prayer circle or serving on the worship evaluation task force. In each case the new member is initiated into the tribe by accepting a specific responsibility by joining an ongoing task group which also functions as a support group for that new member.[12]

A third means of initiating new people into the tribe was identified in the second case study when this long-established and formerly rural congregation was forced to build a new meeting place as a result of its rapid growth. This experience reflects a phenomenon that can be found among all types of churches, *regardless of size. Every new generation of church members appears to feel a compulsion to rebuild the nest.* This rebuilding process may take any one of many different forms. It may be enclosing the outside front steps in an open country church. It may be rebuilding at a new location by a long-established city church. It may be refurbishing the sanctuary in the one hundred year old county seat church. It may be paving the parking lot in the 160-member small town congregation. It may be remodeling the kitchen in another congregation. It may be remodeling an unused room into an office for the new educational assistant in the growing exurban congregation. Regardless of the operational expression of this urge to rebuild the nest, there appears to be a widespread tendency for each new generation of members to feel a need to physically improve the meeting place. In congregations with a stable or slowly declining membership total a new generation of church members may emerge only once every twenty or twenty-five years. In a rapidly growing congregation a new generation comes along every five or six or seven years with a proposal to rebuild the nest.

The important point about this pheonomenon is that it usually represents an opening for initiating new members into the tribe. The decision to remodel or replace or expand the meeting place suddenly creates a need for new committees, additional leaders, more workers and for people to exercise both verbal and nonverbal creative skills. A major fringe benefit of this process, as happened in the second case study described earlier, is the possibility of uniting the longtime members and the newcomers together around a specific, attainable, measurable, visible, satisfying, and unifying goal which enables the newcomers to gain a sense of acceptance and belonging.

Although they differ on substance, parallel methods of initiating newcomers into the tribe can be seen in the congregation which rallies together around a major new missional effort or in the congregation which enlists nearly one-half of the adults in the Bethel series, or in the congregation which undertakes a major financial campaign to pay off the mortgage, or in the congregation where the members, both old and new, gain a sense of unity by surviving a major crisis together, or in the other new ventures which produce that specific, attainable, measurable, visible, satisfying, and unifying goal and which creates the need for additional leaders, more workers, and new skills and competencies.

In conclusion, in addition to recognizing the value of groups to reach and assimilate new members, it is important to understand that becoming a member of a small face-to-face primary group does not automatically make the newcomer gain a sense of belonging or a feeling of acceptance in that congregation. Frequently it is necessary to make a special effort to initiate these newcomers and new groups into that tribe. The alternative is the creation of a series of semi-autonomous and competing cliques.

The Importance of Place[1]

A seven-year-old Chicago resident, who had just moved with his parents to a new apartment, was visiting some old friends a few blocks from where the family had lived for several years. His mother called to tell him that she would be unable to pick him up and he should call a taxi and come home by cab. He called the taxi company, ordered a cab, gave them the address of his former home, hurried over to that apartment building three blocks away where he met the cab and got in, and the taxi drove the seven-year-old to his new home two miles distant. *Why did the seven-year-old meet the taxi at his former home?*

The quality, volume, and degree of participation by those present in congregational singing usually is better with a group of seventy people meeting in a room designed to accommodate eighty to eighty-five worshipers than it is when two hundred persons gather for worship in a sanctuary designed to seat five hundred. *Why?*

Two years after the worst natural disaster in American history—the six billion dollar destruction of Tropical Storm Agnes in 1972—the flood plain of the Wyoming Valley from Corning and Elmira to Wilkes-Barre was being rebuilt as people flocked back in a lemming-like march to return to an area which everyone knows will be flooded again. *Why?*

In a survey of church members, *The Texas Methodist* (November 10, 1972) found that four-fifths of the respondents affirmed the importance of the congregation's physical facilities and two-thirds rejected the viability of a congregation which did not have its own identifiable physical structure. *Why?*

In reporting on a study of how patients in a mental institution are perceived by those in charge, David L. Rosenhan, professor of psychology and law at Stanford University, noted (*Newsweek*, January 29, 1973): "In a psychiatric hospital the place is more important than the person. If you're a patient you must be crazy." *Why?*

In city after city, plans for an expressway have been blocked by those who do not want to move from the homes they have occupied for many years, despite the fact that current legislation makes it financially very attractive for these homeowners to sell and move. *Why?*

When it is was decided to merge the two Mennonite seminaries, one in Chicago and one at Goshen, Indiana, three sites received serious consideration, Chicago, Goshen, and Elkhart, Indiana. *Why was the decision made to move to Elkhart, ten miles from Goshen?*

Every week the bodies of three to four thousand recently deceased persons are transported across a state line for burial. *Why?*

Every day hundreds of thousands of office workers in the city go to the same places for lunch. *Why?*

One method of keeping social order in the city is for residents to carry a mental map of where it is safe to shop, to walk, to play, and to visit. Harvard Professor Stanley Milgrum found that many New Yorkers define a neighborhood in ethnic terms rather than by street boundaries when asked to reproduce their mental map of the city.[2] *Why do people carry these kinds of mental maps in their heads?*

Dr. L. David Mech, a wolf biologist, found that the buffer zones which separate the territorial preserves of various wolf packs are the safest places for deer, and in years when the deer population is small, most of the survivors can be found in these buffer zones.[3] *Why?*

Foreign-born Americans spend more than a quarter of a billion dollars annually visiting the communities in which they were born. *Why?*

The earliest punishments for sin in the Bible include the

expulsion of Adam and Eve from the Garden and the forcing of Cain to be a wanderer and a fugitive. *Why?*

Among the most highly visible remains of the Revolutionary War, the Civil War, World War I, and World War II are battlefields which have become national parks. *Why?*

When more than six families live on the same hall in a public housing apartment building, the crime rate tends to be double that when only four families share the same hall.[4] *Why?*

When it was proposed that the two congregations unite, the members at Cedar Lane Church voted in favor of the merger by a 120 to 2 margin while at Zion Church the proposal was defeated 114 to 8. *Why?*

When asked to wear a name-tag at a meeting, many people write not only their name but also their place of residence on that gummed piece of paper before peeling off the backing and attaching it to their clothing. *Why?*

Christ Church in Hamilton Place, Pennsylvania, is a building shared by two congregations. It has two sets of front doors. The Lutherans use one set and the Reformed members use the other. *Why?*

As the families in the huge Polish community in Chicago move to better housing on the city's fringes, they often pick a home close to Milwaukee Avenue.

"Though I have seen this house and town only twice since 1939, they have always served as reference points and measuring scales for proportions, distance, and values." *Why* would Martin E. Marty, one of the most sophisticated, widely traveled and cosmopolitan of contemporary church leaders write these words as he gazed at a photograph of an old house being moved from Colfax Street in West Point, Nebraska, to a nearby farm?

The answer to all of these questions is that place naturally is important to people, and the more familiar the place, the greater its importance.

The seven-year-old boy naturally gives the cab company the address of a familiar landmark (his former home) when he is seeking to reach a new fixed point. The seven-year-old, and the widely traveled Martin E. Marty, both conceptualize reality in terms of a few fixed geographical places.[5]

The physical design of the meeting place influences people's behavior, and the comfortably full church causes those present to join in the congregational singing while the half-empty sanctuary encourages nonparticipation.

Following destruction by a fire or a flood, people *naturally* want to rebuild on the same ground.[6] People *naturally* tend to sit in the same pew in church Sunday after Sunday.

When the members of a research team arranged to be admitted to various mental institutions, the doctors and the attendants *naturally* believed them to be mentally deranged even though each volunteer on the research team consistently told the truth about himself or herself after admission. Anyone who is a patient in a place for mentally ill persons must be mentally ill. The place declares this to be the truth. (The only ones who suspected the researchers were normal were some of the patients!)

Homeowners, offered the opportunity to sell at a substantial profit, *naturally* prefer to remain in the familiar place rather than move to make room for an expressway.

When two theological seminaries, one General Conference Mennonite and one Mennonite, decided to merge, it soon became apparent to the leaders that the union could be accomplished only if the new seminary was located on a neutral site free of any previous association with either of the two denominational families.[7]

The thousands of families who spend money they cannot afford to take the body of a deceased relative "back home" to be buried are behaving in a *natural and normal* manner in recognizing the importance of death and the place of burial.

When confronted with a proposal to merge their congregation with another and move to the other congregation's meeting place, the members of the threatened congregation *naturally* oppose this plan of action. By contrast it is easy for the members of the other congregation in the proposed merger, who will not have their place of worship changed, to vote for the merger.

When mailed a picture of the house in which he was born and in which he lived for twelve years, a clergyman *naturally* is reminded of his origins and of the base for his perspective in looking at the world, especially when that picture shows the house mounted on a trailer and in the process of being moved from one place to another. One of his basic references points in life is being changed.

From this writer's perspective *the importance of place and space is both one of the most basic factors that must be considered in planning for the role, life, ministry, and program of a worshiping congregation, and also one of the three or four most neglected factors in church planning.*

Before moving on to review some of the reasons for the neglect of this concept and the implications of the concept for church planning, it may be helpful to pause briefly to re-examine this concept, to trace the emergence of this new discipline in some of the pioneering research, and to introduce the reader to some of the literature in the field.

Human Ethology

In academic terms ethology is the discipline directed at the scientific study of animal behavior, and especially of innate relationships to habitat. The pioneering book in the field was published in 1920 by a British businessman and birdwatcher, Henry Eliot Howard. In *Territory in Bird Life* (1920), Howard argued that male birds compete not for females but rather for territory.

The most widely quoted statement on the impact of place on the behavior patterns of people probably belongs to the late Winston Churchill. When Churchill said, "We shape our buildings and afterwards our buildings shape us," he was referring to plans to rebuild the British House of Commons after that structure had been destroyed by German bombers in 1943. He was arguing against the popular semicircular assembly that allows every individual and group to move around the center, and in support of an oblong structure in which the act of crossing from one side of the aisle to the other would require serious deliberation by anyone contemplating a change in his party loyalties. In addition,

Churchill argued against a new meeting place which would be large enough to seat every member of the House of Commons. He strongly preferred a small room which would facilitate easy interruptions and informal interchange and which, by virtue of being seriously overcrowded when major issues were being debated, would reinforce the sense of importance and urgency of these issues.

The academic pioneers of this new science of ethology were Europeans led by Austria's Konrad Lorenz and Holland's Niko Tinbergen. Nearly every significant article and book published in the United States on *human* ethology, with the notable exception of the earliest work of Roger Barker and Herbert F. Wright, has appeared since 1960. The first serious attempt to bring the insights of the new science of human ethology to the attention of planners was a book review essay written by a graduate student studying the health aspects of social policy planning and was published in 1969, while the first serious article on human ethology for planners was not published until 1971.[8]

The discipline of ethology and its relationship to human behavior has been popularized during the past decade by scores of books and articles, several of which have gained a sufficient number of readers to push this concept into the contemporary thinking of planners and to legitimatize placing the word *human* in front of the word *ethology*.

The two books which had the greatest early impact on popularizing this concept were both published in 1966, and the more influential of the two has been Edward T. Hall's *The Hidden Dimension*.[9] Seven years earlier Hall, an anthropologist concerned with training Americans to work overseas, had published *The Silent Language*[10] in which he described the nonverbal language of various cultures. He analyzed how the use of time and spatial relationships are used in communicating feelings and attitudes. In *The Hidden Dimension*, Hall concentrated on man's use of space in an effort "to increase self-identity, intensify experience and decrease alienation . . . to help reintroduce man to himself."

Far greater publicity accompanied the publication in that same year of Robert Ardrey's *The Territorial Imperative*.[11] Ardrey, a playwright turned anthropologist, had gained widespread attention in 1961 with the publication of *African Genesis*. In this second book Ardrey presented a systematic argument that the inherited territorial behavior of animals is also an inherited characteristic of human beings. Ardrey's two books also produced a very strong negative response among academicians.

In 1965 two anthropologists named Tiger and Fox met for the first time at, of all places, the London Zoo, and out of this meeting came the book *The Imperial Animal*.[12] In this pioneering volume the authors speculate on the bonds that hold people together—and the antisocial forces that drive people apart. While they do not speak to such subjects directly, Tiger and Fox help the reader understand why a disproportionately large number of Sunday school teachers are mothers and why it is a good policy for every congregation to have at least one organized group for adult males meeting regularly.

While they began from a radically different perspective, another group of researchers, most notably Roger Barker and his colleagues, has developed a theory that encompasses most of the other work in the field and, to a substantial degree, goes far beyond the other academic pioneers in the field. At first Barker labeled his work "environmental psychology," but later defined it as "ecological psychology."[13] Barker has developed the concept of what he describes as "behavior settings" and argues that physical environment and behavior are inextricably linked together and that the same behavior patterns of human beings keep recurring as individuals return to the same natural behavior setting *and as new people come for the first time to that behavior setting*. There are several difficulties in the path of the person attempting to apply Barker's research to the life of the churches. First, his books are not easy reading! Second, it is a difficult methodology to learn. The method is observational, it requires meticulous and detailed observations, and it involves extensive use of scales and subscales. Third, much of what he has discovered runs counter to conventional wisdom and contradicts some widely cherished traditions of American culture. Finally, his methodology places the primary value on what people actually do in various behavior settings, not on what they say they did or on what others believe they should do. In simple terms, Barker measures and quantifies what people actually do in natural behavior settings rather than theorizing from artificial laboratory experiments.[14]

While Barker's writing has not been directed to a "churchy" audience, his research helps to explain why it probably will be counterproductive for a congregation with an average attendance of two hundred to build a sanctuary seating five hundred in order to accommodate "anticipated future growth" or why the ratio of worship attendance to membership tends to decline as a congregation increases in size or why it is important for the congregation expecting to attract and retain new members to follow the same order of worship week after week or why it is more difficult to recruit lay volunteers in the large congregation than in the small church or why church surveys of members' attitudes and preferences rarely are worth the effort or why laboratory schools for training prospective Sunday school teachers are far less useful than having prospective teachers spend several weeks assisting an experienced teacher.

Most of Barker's research also reinforces several of the distinctions made in the first chapter about the differences between small groups and large groups.

Although they have not attracted a broad lay audience, two volumes by Gerald D. Suttles have had a tremendous influence on professionals concerned with human ethology.[15] In *The Social Order of the Slum*, Suttles conceptualizes the importance of ethnicity and territory in the area around Hull House on Chicago's near West Side. Among the important points for church planners lifted up in this volume, are his definition of the role of the churches to "provide a common establishment where a continuing group of people waive their individuality in favor of their common welfare" and to serve as a clearinghouse or as a bargaining center for temporary and ad hoc solutions to problems.

In his second book Suttles takes on Ardrey, Lorenz, Morris, and the other "territorialists."[16] Although he credits their distinctive contributions, he warns that the sense of territory does not automatically mean that small groups of people cannot be brought together in larger and cohesive groups. He is particularly critical of the emphasis that territoriality breeds aggression. In what he describes as "the ideological overburden" to which the new territorialists have been reacting excessively, he takes issue with the positivistic reductionism which insists that territoriality and aggression are not only inborn traits but also dominant in determining behavior patterns. Suttles insists on a larger and far more complex vision of society. He offers an excellent warning against using any single factor analysis, such as the importance of place in people's lives, as the exclusive route for understanding all facets of life.

While many social scientists, academic figures, authors, and planners were busy debating the theories of the new territorialists and in general explaining how and why they oversimplified the complexity of the real world, others were engaged in developing human ethology to an applied stage in planning, urban design, and human relationships. Marc Fried, for example, followed up Herbert Gans's study of the impact of urban renewal on the people in Boston's West End by describing the bereavement of people displaced from their familiar place.[17] Several of the recently published research reports on the importance of the relationship between human relationships and place and physical space have been brought together in a book edited by Robert Gutman (1972), a sociologist who also lectures to architectural students. This book ranks along with C. M. Deasy's book,[18] Robert B. Bechtel's *Enclosing Behavior*, Anne-Marie Pollowy's *The Urban Nest*,[19] and the Bell, Randall, and Roeder annotated bibliography[20] as the best introductions to the research on human ethology and on the impact of where people live and work on their behavior patterns. Deasy's book may be the best beginning point for the pastor, lay leader, church architect, or denominational executive who is interested in reading further on this subject. Bechtel's *Enclosing Behavior* is another excellent beginning point for further reading. In the introduction to his book Bechtel offers a brief, but comprehensive introduction to the literature in this field. He also discusses the implementation of social goals through the application of research from the behavioral sciences to the process of architectural design in a manner that can be very helpful to the person not professionally trained in architecture.

Deasy contends that physical settings affect us in three different ways: "They influence the stress we experience in accomplishing our group or personal goals. They influence the form and nature of our social contacts. They influence our feelings of identity and self-worth."[21]

While Deasy is excessively influenced by the impact of physical and geographical proximity on the depth of social relationships, he offers a devastating analysis of the nonverbal communication by banks to potential customers before the design of bank buildings began to be influenced by the behavioral sciences. Banks and savings and loan associations have begun to apply Deasy's insights, but few churches reflect the same level of understanding of how the design of a structure can attract or repel first-time visitors to that place.

From an entirely different academic perspective John Cassel, of the School of Public Health at the University of North Carolina, has examined the impact of crowding and high densities on stress.[22] Cassel concluded that four principles can be deduced to explain the impact of crowding on human beings. First, crowding may not produce social disorganization, but it tends to facilitate it. Second, not all members of a group being crowded will be equally vulnerable to the effects of crowding, and the most dominant individuals will show the least effect while the most severe effects will be felt by the least dominant. (This means that church buildings can be designed by church leaders to cause shy, bashful, and timid people to stay away.) Third, the two critical buffers which may reduce the effects of crowding are (1) the biological capacity of all organisms to adapt to new surroundings and (2) the group support of the family. (This means the church building designed for families may repel single adults!) Fourth, the consequences of social disorganization are not to be measured in terms of specific illnesses but rather in the increased susceptibility to disease in general.[23]

Perhaps the most widely publicized application of the insights from the discipline of human ethology have been in the contributions of Oscar Newman.[24] Newman contends that it is possible to design crime-free urban housing. Among his many observations and recommendations are: (1) it is important to recognize the distinction between density (dwelling units per acre) and the height of the building in predicting the crime rate; (2) the age and family composition of apartment dwellers influence the recommendations for the height and density of public housing; (3) the size of the apartment project, as well as its location, is an influential factor in predicting the crime rate; and (4) good planning does *not* result simply in moving crime from one neighborhood to another. Newman contends that good planning eliminates the *opportunity* for crime. Newman, for example, was the first to point out that when only four apartments open on a corridor, the residents of all four apartments will be concerned with what happens in that hallway, but when six apartments open on a corridor, the tendency is for none of the residents to display that same level of concern about that shared space.

Two of the most influential books on the impact of place and physical setting on attitudes and behavior are the products of a psychologist, Robert Sommer.[25] Dominance, the deference pyramid, territoriality, the relationship between space and status, leadership, the implications of privacy, the importance of personalizing space, and user behavior are among the subjects Sommer discusses in his first book. Sommer moves to a much more critical tone and strongly denounces the effects of people and interpersonal relationships of "hard" architecture.[26]

The changing methods which a new urban dweller uses to create a new "home territory" are described by sociologist Lyn H. Lofland[27] who analyzes the impact local customs, personal traditions, and territory have on order in the city filled with people who do not know one another. She is very helpful in describing how public places come to be identified in distinctive ways so that nearly everyone recognizes his or her place, and how this tends to be an everchanging pattern, thus explaining why the person who returns after an absence does not feel "at home" in what once was a familiar place.

Another book, useful to church leaders, comes from this same stream and analyzes the "pecking order" in human society.[28] Written in nontechnical language, this volume is a useful addition to one aspect of human ethology. The longest chapter, "How Dominance Is Signaled," is perhaps the easiest to translate into an understanding of how ecclesiastical gatherings function.

Why the Neglect?

While the effort here has been to lift up for attention only the more prominent books and articles in the field of human ethology, even this list is sufficiently long to prompt some people to ask why the implications of this subject have been almost totally neglected by church planners. To respond to that question moves the discussion to the speculative level, but that subject may justify a few paragraphs.

The most obvious reason probably is that the science of ethology and its application for the attitudes and behavior patterns of human beings has emerged only recently. It is doubtful if those who graduated from college before 1966 or 1967 would have been exposed to the subject unless subsequent to 1966 they were enrolled in a graduate school of sociology or anthropology or perhaps one of the design sciences or unless they carried on a systematic continuing education program following graduation.

Second, community planners long have made extensive use of maps, and this dependence has been picked up by many church planners. The spotting on a map of the location of church buildings and of the places of residence of people may be less than useless since it suggests relationships that may be completely irrelevant, but it is easy to accomplish and often is very fulfilling for both the person doing it and for those viewing the finished product.

Third, many people have had tremendous difficulty in transferring the implications of the research carried out with birds, fish, and mammals to human beings. The assumption that one can generalize about the instincts, attitudes, and behavior patterns of human beings from research on animals has been rejected by many anthropologists, sociologists, planners, preachers, and theologians.[29] This may be the most decisive single factor in the neglect of this discipline by church planners. Theology and ethology often look at the behavior patterns of human beings from substantially different perspectives! The theologians tend to emphasize the professional perspective while the behavioralists tend to emphasize the relational dimensions of life.

Fourth, a part of the answer to this question on neglect can be found in the science of human ethology. Outside observers frequently project what they define as "rational behavior" and comment critically on the divergence between the projected rational behavior and the actual, observable behavior patterns. The science of ethology suggests that this projection of rational behavior may be extremely simplistic and ignore other important factors. An example of the return of former residents and businessmen to the flood plain of the Wyoming Valley is an example of this. What is really "rational behavior"? To return to familiar places or to pioneer in a new and unfamiliar place?

The science of human ethology suggests that the predictable and natural behavior pattern is for flooded-out victims to rebuild on the flood plain, for burned-out congregations to rebuild at the old location despite the complete absence of off-street parking, and for church planners who have developed a style and system with which they are comfortable to continue with that style and system—thus continuing to ignore the implications of a relatively new science such as human ethology.

Finally, the research findings of many of the people concerned with human ethology and environmental psychology are ignored because they focus on the observed behavior patterns of people rather than on the wants and needs of the leaders and decision-makers. Perhaps the outstanding example of this is the large and impressive quantity of research that suggests, from the perspective of the students, a high school should not include more than five hundred students.[30] A high school that small, however, cannot satisfy the wants and needs of many teachers, athletic coaches, school administrators, architects, guidance counselors, and other professional specialists. Therefore, for the past four decades the trend has been in the direction of larger high schools to provide better employment opportunities for specialists. The researchers in human ethology have failed to identify with an influential client.

An interesting parallel in the churches is the value placed on bigness, despite the impressive evidence that suggests the participation of the members decreases as the congregation increases in size (see pages 50-52). Many of the most influential leaders in the churches, however, find their needs are met more adequately by large congregations, and thus the "reward system" in most denominations reinforces the belief that bigger is better.

What Are Those Implications?

Perhaps the most highly visible and widely known expression of human ethology in twentieth-century religious terms is the modern Zionist movement founded by Theodor Herzl in 1897. This movement can be understood more adequately if it is viewed as an expression of territoriality as well as an expression of religious needs.

The parish church in American Christianity offers an opportunity for applying principles of human ethology in order to understand the dynamics of congregational behavior. Historically, the parish church has had three distinctive expressions in the United States. The one most frequently referred to is the congregation which serves most of the residents of a geographically defined neighborhood or community. This expression of the parish church still can be seen in a diminishing proportion of Roman Catholic parishes (both urban and rural), in a growing number of rural Hutterite and Amish congregations, and in a decreasing number of rural Lutheran parishes. When studied, these parishes frequently bring to mind Christopher Morley's comment: "To be rooted in a place that has meaning is perhaps the best gift a child can have."

The second expression of the parish church which can be perceived more clearly with the insights from human ethology is the nationality parish. Again, place is very important. But in this case the boundaries of the parish are not defined by geographical lines; rather they are defined by language, nationality, kinship, friendship, and ethnic ties. The place where people meet, the parish church building, gives a physical substance to these intangible ties which bind people together. The building is a response to the need for a sense of place.

The third expression of the parish church can be described most accurately today as "the ex-neighborhood church."[31] Too often the outside expert perceives this as a congregation which once served the people living around the meeting place and urges that a major effort be made to return to that pattern by "serving this community." A better beginning point in planning for the future ministry of this type of congregation is to define the characteristics of the current membership rather than to try to turn back the pages on the calendar. A common example of this is the congregation which was founded to serve the residents of a specific geographically defined neighborhood. Today, most of these are either dead or have moved out of the neighborhood. The children and grandchildren of these members, plus the spouses of these members, constitute the core of today's leadership. Today, this is clearly not a parish church in the traditional terms of a geographically defined parish. Frequently, however, this focus on a geographical neighborhood has been replaced by (1) the need for many members to return to this familiar place to worship God, to renew and reinforce friendship and kinship ties, and to actively express their religious commitment to this fellowship as well as to God, and (2) the emergence of a specialized ministry to one slice of the population spectrum. The most common expression of this specialized ministry is to lonely and mature widowed women. Formerly, the evangelistic outreach of this congregation was built around its central strength, the ministry to a geographical neighborhood. Today, the best approach to expressing its evangelistic outreach also should be built around its strength, not around its weakness. This may be a ministry to lonely, elderly persons without regard to their place of residence. To plan for the future by building on weakness and alienation is almost certain to produce frustration. The science of human ethology can help define the strengths and assets of this expression of the parish church rather than to focus on attempts to recreate yesterday or to "fill holes" or to build on weaknesses.

Closely related to this—but a different application of the insights of human ethology—is the case of the 700-member congregation which relocated its meeting place from the central business district. After constructing a new meeting place in a suburban residential neighborhood, the leaders began to wonder why the congregation was not increasing in numbers. After all, a basic reason for the relocation had been to provide new opportunities for evangelistic outreach and growth. There are scores of families in this neighborhood who have no active relationship to any worshiping congregation. Why are they not flocking to unite or at least to visit "our church"? In ethological terms this relocated congregation frequently appears to residents already living in the neighborhood to be an independent and self-sufficient alien in a strange land. The act of relocation does not produce a sense of territoriality. The relocated congregation frequently is perceived by the residents as an intruder in an already established set of relationships in that place.

In what are not completely unrelated circumstances, human ethology also speaks to the group-building processes in the church. The opportunity for the group to alter the existing environment is an important element in the process of developing a sense of community. This is one of the basic insights gleaned from the science of human ethology. It helps explain why the youth fellowship, which at the moment is simply a loose collection of individuals, wants to repaint and decorate the room set aside for their meetings. Some of them *know* this will help turn these young people, many of whom are new to this organization, into a more cohesive group. This also helps to explain why three or four years later the next generation of high school youth show little interest in that particular room. It is not *their* place!

This insight also helps to explain why each new generation of church members feels an urge to rebuild the nest (see pages 62-63). In addition to being an important assimilation process, it also is a natural means of passing control from one generation to another generation of members. A very common parallel, which also is explained by human ethology, is for the wife of the newly arrived pastor to want to have a voice in choosing the paint and wallpaper to be used in redecorating the parsonage. The church leaders who insist that it would be easier and more efficient to redecorate the parsonage or manse before the arrival of the new minister, while the house is unoccupied, are ignoring these scientific insights.

This same basic human attachment to "our place" helps to explain why that older adult Sunday school class, which spearheaded the refurbishing of the church lounge, resists the arguments of the Board of Christian Education that this class move to another room in order to allow the lounge to be used by the larger young couples class. Which side is using "rational" arguments in this case?

This insight helps to explain why the small congregation which relocated in a residential neighborhood from its near-downtown location grew so rapidly following relocation. The assets were too limited and the members too few for it to build immediately. Therefore, they met in a school for a year while (1) some members were building face-to-face relationships with unchurched residents as part of the evangelistic outreach effort, and (2) other members began the building-planning and financing process. Subsequently, the alteration of the physical environment was a group-building effort, by both the "old-timers" who were a part of the relocation process and the new members who united with the congregation after its relocation.

The serious student of human ethology also can understand the surprise and frustration which followed implementation of the decision to house Lutheran, Roman Catholic, and Presbyterian theological seminaries on one already completed campus. First, alteration of the physical environment already had been completed, and so construction of the new campus could not be a group-building process. Second, he knew that rank was more important than physical proximity in the degree of contact among faculty members. Third, arrangements for coffee breaks and other social meetings were inhibited by the building design, and, therefore, these would tend to be alienating rather than unifying events. Fourth, each faculty member had a "territory" (academic courses and identification as a specialist) to protect, and, therefore, it would be difficult to have significant cross-registration in parallel courses. Fifth, since there are three denominational territories to guard, their distinctive processes for overseeing the theological education of future clergy would work against rather than in support of academic cooperation. Sixth, a student of human ethology could recognize that the deference pyramids had already been established within each seminary and that these would accentuate the vertical relationships within the individual seminaries while weakening the horizontal relationships across institutional and denominational barriers. Finally, it could be predicted that the students, who would be newer, would have less sense of territory and fewer institutional ties, and would be open to cross registration; but that the institutional, architectural, and faculty barriers would have to be encouraging and supportive for this to happen on any significant scale.

Another growing pattern in American society can also be understood in terms of people's attachment to place. The family that buys its first recreational vehicle usually wants to travel. They tend to be wandering vagabonds. If they trade it in later for another recreational vehicle or "house on wheels," the common tendency is to seek a secure place to park it. One result is a rapid increase in the number of vacation sites which sell small parcels of land to owners of recreational vehicles. The buyers want the assurance of a familiar and secure place for their vacations.

The science of human ethology also helps people understand why the newer seating arrangements at airports often are in units of three or in pairs with a wide tray between two seats. Strangers want to stake out their own turf and to have adequate space around them. Church leaders often have difficulty, however, in transferring this concept into designing the seating arrangements in a house of worship. Too often the seating arrangement is designed for symmetry, visual appeal, or to look good on a church bulletin, a picture postcard, or the cover of a magazine rather than to accommodate strangers. The stranger who comes to church naturally is inclined to choose a seat at the end of the pew. But, if he comes early to insure a seat at the end of the pew, he knows he may have to surrender it to latecomers or tolerate people climbing over his legs to reach the interior places in the pew. The individual, who may be a longtime member of that congregation, finds it more attractive to attend an adult Sunday school class where each chair is independent of the others and where he can stake out his claim to some comfortable privacy and then go home instead of attending corporate worship. Or he may decide to stay away completely on Sunday morning.

This new science of human ethology can help church leaders understand why a white Lutheran pastor, who was assigned to a "street ministry" in the black ghetto of Cleveland's near east side in the early 1960s, soon discovered that he had to rent a small storefront to serve as an office. Being white was one handicap. Not having an identifiable place to which he was institutionally related was a second handicap which would have made his assignment impossible unless he had been willing to recognize the importance of territory and place.

The science of human ethology helps people understand why the "New Army" offers private rooms in the barracks, why the teen-ager insists on keeping the door to his or her room closed, why commuters prefer to drive alone in their own car to work rather than to ride a bus, why one of the attractive elements so prominently displayed in the advertising of new apartment buildings is the guarantee of privacy, and why one of the most effective methods of developing a corps of happy Sunday school teachers is to guarantee each one that his or her room will not be used by any other group or for any other activity during the week.

An understanding of the importance of place in the lives of people helps to explain the popularity of the hymn "How Blessed Is This Place" and why the ultimate punishment in "The Man Without a Country" was to bar the central figure from ever being able to hear about or read about the United States or to be able to set foot on the shores of his native land.

The new insights which have emerged from the behavioral sciences during the last dozen years make it easier to understand the reasons behind the design of new bank buildings and shopping centers. They are deliberately designed to make it easier for individuals to drive to the bank or shopping center, park, and go in to transact their business. Contrast this with the congregation which meets in a building designed for pedestrian traffic coming in from the sidewalk next to the street and which subsequently builds a parking lot beside or behind the church building, yet which never identifies the "right" entrance to be used by persons coming into the building from the parking lot and which refuses to "deface" the walls of the interior with signs that would direct a stranger from one part of the building to another activity.

Despite the volume of material that has been published on the importance of place in the lives of people, several denominations fail to include this as a factor in their planning for small congregations. Instead of affirming the importance of the familiar place in the lives of people, a great variety of proposals are developed which emphasize such factors as potential congregational mergers, adequate salary for a minister, a "viable size," an adequate program, a larger financial base, lower expenditures for the maintenance of meeting places, and better utilization of both volunteer and paid leadership. Frequently, these goals clash with the sense of territory and the attachment to place, and the result of months of planning is an impasse.

Another subject in church planning which usually disregards the insights from human ethology is the contemporary passion for flexibility in building design. The multi-purpose room which can be used by many different groups for a variety of uses is an important goal in the design of many new church buildings. Occasionally, it is achieved—as is illustrated by First-Wayne Street United Methodist Church in Fort Wayne. More often, however, the results parallel what happened with the plans of the School Construction System Development team in California. After several years of use in ten schools, it was found that a majority of the teachers were not even aware of the flexibility built into the design. Less than one-fourth of the teachers in these ten schools had been involved in any alteration of their teaching space which utilized the flexibility built into the physical design of the building.[32]

Returning to the subject of the relocation of churches from one neighborhood to a new site, the observations of Cassel and Maclay and Knipe become relevant. The proposed relocation tends to be initiated and carried through by a few dominant families and often is resisted by subordinate individuals who lack both group and family support systems. Who are the casualties in this process? Precisely the people who would be identified in advance by the ethologist to whom this question was presented. Those people who most need the support of the familiar place tend to be the ones who are least influential in the decision-making process on merger or relocation. What does the Christian ethic say to this?

Today literally millions of Christians will gladly share with a listener the story of their religious pilgrimage. The climax of the story is when the person describes how he or she came to accept Jesus Christ as a personal savior. Usually this event is linked with a specific physical place as well as a particular point in time. This is consistent with the Biblical account of how God revealed himself to man, including the encounter with Adam in the Garden of Eden, with Moses on Mount Horeb, with Isaiah in the temple at Jerusalem, and on through the Old Testament and the New Testament including Paul's frequent reference to when Jesus spoke to him on the road to Damascus. In each case the place becomes an important part of understanding God's revelation.

Perhaps the most important general application of the science of human ethology concerns the call to mission. During the past fifteen years the exhortation from the pulpit repeatedly has been the challenge to go forth in mission. The call to go on the pilgrimage, to venture forth on faith, to leave the old behind, and to welcome the new are themes which have been emphasized in an untold number of sermons preached during the 1960s and 1970s.

It is at this point the insights of human ethology, the lessons from the Old Testament, and the teachings of Jesus converge. As Dr. Paul Tournier has pointed out in his excellent book on this subject, it is to those who already have a place that God sends the call to move on.[33] Each individual needs to find a home before he can leave. Many of those who proclaim the challenge to others to follow them in mission, already have found a home in their calling, their profession, their denominational family, their cause, and/or their denominational machinery. They may overlook the fact that those they are asking to go forth in mission have not yet found a place. Many who are listening to this challenge came to hear words of guidance and inspiration in their quest for a home, in their longing for a faith which can sustain them in this pilgrimage, in their search for a vision of what could be and of what God has in store for them. They came to hear the Gospel and instead heard what they perceived as a sermon on the Law. In contrast to the Bible, this proclamation on the Law overlooked the importance of place in people's lives.

Two Basic Distinctions

In addition to these general applications of the importance of place in the lives and behavior patterns of people, it may be helpful to lift up several more specific applications of the concept. Before doing that, however, two basic distinctions require elaboration. The first of these is to distinguish between community, which the University of Chicago's school of sociologists of the 1920s defined with a heavy emphasis on geography, and an individual's attachment to a particular place. For example, the sense of belonging to a rural German Lutheran parish in central Wisconsin can be described in terms of human ethology and the concepts developed by Robert Park and his associates at the University of Chicago during the second and third decades of this century.[34] By contrast, the fact that a fifty-three-year-old man, a lifelong member of that rural church, has been sitting next to the aisle in the third pew from the rear on the left-hand side of the nave for the past three decades can best be described in terms of human ethology or an attachment to a particular place or territoriality. Membership in that religious community and attachment to place in that pew are related and overlapping, but different subjects in this discussion. Human ecology is an attempt to systematize our understandings about the larger constellation of people, institutions, environment, and territory. Human ethology is an attempt to focus on the more narrowly defined relationships of a person or a family or a small group of people to a specific place.

The second of these two basic distinctions is directed at the difference between the individual's *attachment* to a particular place and how that attachment influences behavior patterns and the overlapping concept developed by Roger G. Barker in his concept of "behavior setting."[35] Barker is primarily concerned with identifying the various factors which constitute a behavior setting and the impact of these upon the behavior patterns of people. The behavior setting is the independent variable in his experiments, and the behavior of the people is the dependent variable. One behavior setting elicits one set of behavior patterns, while a different behavior setting produces a different set of behavior patterns. For example, churchgoers socialize on the sidewalk but stop talking when they enter the sanctuary. This is true of both the longtime members and also of the first-time visitors. On entering the sanctuary, however, the longtime member usually automatically goes to that pew which represents "my place," while the stranger pauses and looks around for a vacant place.

Operational Applications

Now that the academic differences distinguishing human ethology from human ecology and ecological psychology have been disposed of, it may be useful to suggest a dozen different operational applications of the insights derived from all three disciplines.

1. First, anyone taking seriously the insights from human ethology will be able to affirm the value of setting apart a specially designed room for the primary purpose of coming together for the corporate worship of God. While some critics may protest that it is inefficient or uneconomical to spend all that money on an expensive room that is used only a few hours each week, these arguments overlook the historical importance of place in the life of the Christian community and in the lives of individuals. That special room for the corporate worship of God also becomes a very influential behavior setting.

2. Second, if the insights of human ethology are combined with

the characteristics of large groups described in chapter 1, it should be apparent that a useful general rule is the larger the size of an adult Sunday school class and/or the older the members of that class (the attachment to place tends to increase with age), the more important it is that each class have its own regular meeting room rather than be expected to move from room to room every few months. In other words, it is best not to shuffle classes every few months. The move to a different meeting room not only weakens the unifying factor of the common attachment to a familiar place, it also means a move to a new behavior setting and the disruption created by a new set of expected patterns of behavior.

3. When the common characteristics of large groups are combined with the normal human attachment to place, it should be obvious that it is counterproductive to expect regular churchgoers to (a) sit in different places every week "in order to meet more people" or (b) occupy the front pews or (c) leave the back pews vacant for latecomers and visitors.

4. One of the most effective means of encouraging longer pastorates, of increasing the probability of a happy marriage for "our pastor," and of reinforcing positive attitudes among the pastor's children is to pay a housing allowance to the minister rather than to provide a parsonage or manse. This will enable the minister's family to have "our own place."

5. If two or more congregations are served by one pastor and if housing is to be supplied to the minister, it is better for the parsonage to be owned by one congregation rather than to have it jointly owned by two or three congregations.

6. If the insights of human ethology and ecological psychology are combined with the differences between large groups and small groups, it becomes apparent that the following values and goals will tend not to be reinforced in those large congregations which attempt to operate as "one big family" but usually will receive substantial reinforcement in small congregations and in those large churches which place a strong emphasis on the group life of the congregation.[36]

(a) Members will be absent less frequently.

(b) Members will participate voluntarily more frequently.

(c) More members will demonstrate more leadership behavior.

(d) More members will be involved in more greetings and social transactions with other members.

(e) Members will affirm the value and importance of their own participation more often and to a greater degree.

(f) Members will have fewer difficulties and frustrations with the internal communication system of the parish.

(g) Members will function in positions of responsibility more frequently.

(h) Members will display a strong sense of congregational cohesiveness.

7. If the goal is to have the persons present for worship leave directly following the worship service, the building should be designed with a direct and unobstructed corridor from the narthex to the parking lot. If the goal is to encourage people to linger for a fellowship period following corporate worship, the natural exit from the sanctuary should lead into a large open fellowship area which will encourage socialization. The design of the structure should reflect the values and goals of the congregation, not the design of some other structure!

8. The larger the congregation, the smaller the proportion of teen-agers who will be actively involved in most of the opportunities for participation available to youth. The larger the congregation, the weaker the parental influence on the behavior patterns of the youth. The smaller the congregation (or "the place"), the larger the proportion of the teen-agers who will realize important satisfactions resulting from developing a competence or being challenged or being involved as a member of that congregation, rather than only as a member of a subgroup of that congregation or being valued by other people or gaining moral, religious, and cultural values or having their self-confidence reinforced. In other words, the nature of the "place," "the behavior setting," and the size of the congregation should be major factors in designing a ministry to youth and in the subsequent evaluation of that ministry.

9. The minister who has moved from serving as the pastor of a small congregation to become the pastor of a large congregation

normally will feel serious reservations about the quality of the internal communication system within that large congregation and *normally* will be alarmed about the impact of rumors. This is a *normal* response to changing from one type of place or behavior setting where the internal communication process is comparatively simple and open and where the grapevine usually is a positive reinforcement of that internal communication system, to a new and far more complex behavior setting where much of the internal communication does not touch the pastor directly, where the grapevine is more likely to be a negative factor, and where a comparatively large proportion of the members are relatively uninformed on any specific issue.

10. The research coming from the discipline of human ethology, in contrast to the research of the rural sociologists of the 1920s who emphasized a geographical definition of community, suggests it is counterproductive to attempt to make church members feel guilty because they are not members of that congregation which has a meeting place close to their place of residence.

11. The large congregation meeting in a large and complex building and which also places a high priority on a ministry to young children will affirm the importance of place in a child's life by making the three-year-olds' room for this year the four-year-olds' room for next year, the five-year-olds' room for the following year and the first grade room for the year after that, rather than moving the children from room to room every year. The importance of that familiar place is very great to this age group. It is unrealistic to expect the young child to be able to form a mental map of a large and complex building at age four or five or six. Changing the behavior setting every year will tend to be a disruptive factor.

In those congregations where tradition is more important than young children, a compromise may be to place permanent strips of colored tape on the floor leading from the entrances to the various rooms for young children. The strip of red tape, for example, could lead from the entrance to the room for two-year-olds. The green tape could lead to the three-year-olds' room, the yellow tape to the room for four-year-olds, and the blue tape to the room for five-year-old children. This will help the young child conceptualize the relationship between familiar point A (the entrance used by that family) and familiar point B (the room used by that age group).

12. Perhaps the most complex operational implication of the importance of place in people's lives can be identified by two broad sweeping generalizations, which obviously do not apply to all individuals nor to all congregations. First, the attachment to place is stronger among the members of small congregations than it is among the members of large congregations. Second, the large congregation usually is more dependent on the pastor than is the small congregation.

What does that mean in everyday terms? It suggests that long pastorates are far more important in large congregations, where the sense of continuity is in the pastor, than in small congregations where the continuity rests more heavily in that familiar meeting place and in the relationships of the people to one another. It suggests that it is far easier for the pastor serving a large congregation to slip into a highly paternalistic leadership role than it is for the pastor of a small congregation. It suggests that when a merger of two small congregations is being considered, the decision on the permanent meeting place is far more important than the decision on the identity of the next pastor. It suggests that an effective strategy for undermining the strength of a denomination would be to encourage (a) the merger of small churches and (b) short (three to six years or less) pastorates for ministers serving large congregations. It suggests that the minister who is strongly opposed to a paternalistic role and the dependency which accompanies paternalism, should either (a) avoid serving large congregations or (b) develop a high level of competence in the effective management of large groups of people. [37] It also suggests that serving as the pastor of a series of small congregations is not necessarily appropriate preparation for serving as the pastor of a large congregation. In other words, size and the varying importance of different persons' attachment to a familiar place are two of the characteristics that can be used to distinguish one type of congregation from other types of churches.

These are only a few of the many specific operational applications of these concepts, but they should illustrate the relevance of the subject to church planning. The only programmatic area in the churches where the importance of place has been widely recognized has been in Christian education, although rarely in the design of buildings for Christian education. Unfortunately, the dominant architectural trend has been to design buildings to house classes rather than to design places which encourage learning.

In these first two chapters an extensive effort has been made to suggest that two of the most important, and also two of the most neglected, factors in church planning are (a) the differences in behavior patterns between large groups and small groups of people and (b) the attachment of people to physical place and how the nature of that behavior setting influences people's behavior. In a parallel manner the choice of the planning model to be used also has a tremendous impact on the nature of the recommendations coming out of any planning effort, and that is the subject of the next chapter.

3

Which Planning Model?

Readers born and reared on a farm during the first four decades of this century probably know what a threshing machine is. For those who did not have that priceless experience, a threshing machine was a large box on wheels which could be moved from farm to farm. Farmers would pitch bundles of oats in one end of it, and the machine would blow straw out the other end. Or they could put bundles of wheat or barley in one end, and the machine would blow straw out the other. It really did not matter what you put into the threshing machine at one end; it still blew straw out the other end.

Some farmers used another machine called an ensilage cutter or, more commonly, a silo filler. Farmers would place bundles of corn in one end of that machine, and it blew silage up into the silo from the other end. Some farmers put alfalfa hay in one end of that machine and got silage out the other end. Occasionally a farmer accidentally placed his hand in one end of that machine, and it produced a small quantity of high-protein silage out the other end.

One machine was designed to produce straw, the other to produce silage. This analogy can be carried over to approaches to planning. The approach used in planning is the most significant single factor in determining the outcome. The choice of the model to be used will have a major impact in determining the nature of the recommendations produced. Frequently the choice of a model will be more influential than the nature of the data that are gathered. Or, to be more precise, the choice of the planning model also will determine the nature of the data to be collected.

For example, the model most widely used by professionals in the churches can be described very simply as a church and community planning model. This approach calls for a study of the membership of that congregation and a study of the geographical community surrounding the meeting place of that congregation. Basically it is a rural sociology approach based on the premise that community can be defined in geographical terms and the assumption that every congregation should minister to the people living near the meeting place. When that planning model is used by churches today, it usually produces several predictable outcomes, including these four. First, it will be discovered that that congregation does not serve many of the residents who live in the vicinity of the meeting place. Second, it will be suggested that unless that congregation begins to develop a stronger outreach to the people living near the meeting place, it will die. Third, the church and community planning model usually produces at least a few recommendations about the meeting place such as the need to remodel or to add parking or perhaps even to relocate to a new and more hospitable site. Fourth, the use of this planning model usually will produce a report that highlights the weaknesses, liabilities, and shortcomings of the congregation using that particular planning model.

These comments should *not* be misconstrued as criticism of the church and community planning model. They are simply descriptive statements. A threshing machine will produce straw regardless of whether bundles of oats or barley or wheat or rye are being fed into the machine. An ensilage cutter will produce silage, regardless of whether corn or alfalfa hay is being fed into the machine. The church and community planning model usually will produce those four predictable outcomes. The PBE (planning-budgeting-evaluation) planning model usually produces recommendations on church finances. The use of a church-growth planning model usually will produce recommendations on evangelism, new member recruitment, and improved assimilation of new members. The use of a social action planning model will produce recommendations on greater community involvement by that congregation, an increased allocation of financial resources to service ministries, the allocation of staff time to community affairs, and increased use of the building by neighborhood organizations.

The basic thesis of this chapter is that there is no such thing as a neutral planning approach. Every approach to planning and every planning model has its own built-in biases. Therefore the most critical decision in any planning effort is not in the data-gathering effort, but rather in the choice of the planning model that will be used to process the data. If you want to produce a big pile of straw, rent a threshing machine, and pitch bundles of oats or wheat or barley into the machine. If you want to fill a silo, do not rent a threshing machine, find a silo filler. Likewise, if you want specific recommendations on recruiting new members, use a church-growth planning model, not a church and community planning model. If, however, you want some recommendations on real estate, the church and community planning model may be a wise choice.

Therefore, the first factor to be considered in any planning effort is to recognize that the choice of a planning model will have a tremendous impact on the nature of the recommendations that result from that venture. This can be illustrated even more clearly by looking at the next three issues that should be considered in choosing a planning model. The first of these three issues can be described by listening in on three pairs of conversations.

Winners or Losers?

"Our basic problem is the age of our people," commented an influential lay member of Bethel Church. "Well over one-half of our members have passed their fiftieth birthday, and at least a third are in their sixties or older. We only have a handful of active members in the twenty-five to forty age bracket, so I don't see a very bright future for our church. The young couples of today are the backbone of tomorrow's church, and we simply don't have them! We're an old congregation in an old building in an old neighborhood with no future."

"I know I'm enjoying myself more here than any place I ever served," exclaimed the Rev. James Lee of the Westside Church.

"This is the oldest congregation I've ever pastored, but it's also the most vital and evangelistic. Westside was started in 1923 to serve a new residential neighborhood that developed out here after World War I. It peaked in size and strength in the early 1950s, but as people kept moving farther out and as new churches were started in the suburbs, Westside began to decline. It reached bottom in the late 1960s when a major effort to bring in more young couples was unsuccessful. When I came in 1974, it was with the clear understanding that the evangelistic outreach would be concentrated on older couples, mature, single adults, widows, widowers, and others who feel neglected, passed by, and overlooked by the world in general and the church in particular."

"What's happened since you arrived?" was the next question addressed to this enthusiastic forty-nine-year-old minister.

"When I arrived here back in 1974, it seemed to me that we had an obvious match between a great need and a tremendous bundle of resources," came the reply. "As the years passed, this neighborhood has aged. With the exception of the apartment buildings, all the houses are fifty to seventy years old. As the housing has grown older, so have the people. The grade school directly across the street from our church was closed in 1968 because of the lack of kids. About four years ago the junior high school serving this community was converted into a branch for the community college, and the kids are bussed to a new, middle school five miles from here. In 1970 the median age of the population in the eight census tracts surrounding our church building was 51.7 years.

"Over half of our members are past sixty years of age. We have 119 widows, widowers, or divorced persons out of a membership of 417," continued the Rev. Mr. Lee. "That means we have a lot of longtime members who have been members of Westside for thirty or forty years. There is a tremendous amount of loyalty. This also means we have a lot of retired people who have the time to give to volunteer work in the church. These people really love the Lord and their church. Most of our members have experienced a lot of grief and sorrow and trouble, and so they know how to relate to people who are lonely or hurt or alienated or sick or in trouble.

WHICH PLANNING MODEL?

When we first began this evangelistic mission to mature adults, there were still some who thought that we should try one more time to reach more young couples with children; but as these folks got involved in ministry to people a lot like themselves, they began to believe that God has a special mission for Westside Church.

"We've had five major assets that have made this whole thing work," continued Rev. Lee in explanation to a stranger of what was happening in this congregation. "Clearly, the first is the Christian commitment of our people. Anyone with a weak commitment has dropped out or transferred to another church years ago. Second, we have six strong adult Sunday school classes. One is for men. That's mostly widowers, husbands whose wives are shut-ins, bachelors, and men who have been in that same men's class since it was formed in the late 1920s. We have three women's classes. The oldest is the counterpart of the men's class. A second one we started three years ago for widowed women, and the third we started last year for newcomers and women who weren't in any class. Most of the women in this newest class are in their fifties and sixties, and they're all employed outside the home.

"Two years ago we started a fourth class for empty-nesters (couples who have seen their youngest child leave home). It now includes several widows and widowers. Three years ago we started a Sunday school class for single parents. About a third of the people are men, and it's our fastest growing class. With a couple of exceptions, the only active members we have who are under forty are in that single-parent class. Next month we're starting another new class for people who are new in this community. I expect it will be largely another widows' class, but we have two couples and one widowed man, all in their middle sixties, who have agreed to organize it.

"Our third asset here," explained Mr. Lee as he led his guest into a large classroom, "is that every one of the classes and groups has a major mission project which gives the members a sense of outreach. It keeps their focus on the needs of people beyond our membership, offers many different opportunities for involvement by people who aren't very competent in verbal skills but can use their hands. And, of course, any group which has a project

97

requiring the use of creative skills is usually an open group that welcomes newcomers. Working on the group or class project helps the newcomers feel accepted.

"Our fourth assest," continued Mr. Lee as he led his guest through the fifty-three-year-old white frame structure, "is the building. It's old enough that no one objects to a nail in the wall. It's kind of expensive to heat in the winter, but that's a small price to pay for all the hassels we don't have. Finally, our members are a tremendous asset. As I mentioned earlier, they've lived through a lot. The imminence of death is real for most of them; they have a tremendous Christian commitment; they're loyal; a lot of them have plenty of free time to be personally involved in ministry to others; and they love one another. We don't have a social class system that would cause people living around here to feel they wouldn't fit in here at Westside."

"Our problem is our location," observed the minister of Old First Church downtown. "We've dropped in membership from 1700 in 1955 to less than half that today. We used to average between 800 and 900 in Sunday school week after week; last Sunday it was 232. Years ago, downtown was the ideal location for a church, but not today! The movement of the people to the suburbs, the traffic congestion downtown, opening of the shopping centers, the establishment of all those new suburban congregations with new, one-story buildings, the lack of off-street parking, the rise in the rate of crime, the obsolete buildings, and the economic decline of the central business district means the end of an era for the downtown church."

"We couldn't do what we're doing if we didn't have this downtown location," categorically declared the pastor of Central Church. "Since 1970 our average attendance at worship on Sunday morning has climbed from 201 to 378, our Sunday school has more than doubled, we have added two program staff members, and our choir has quadrupled. We're three blocks from the interchange which ties the east-west expressway to the north-south freeway. That means three-fourths of the population is within fifteen minutes of our meeting place on Sunday morning. While it may take two or three times that long to get back and forth during the evening rush hour, we don't schedule many things to conflict with that traffic.

"Our whole program and ministry is directed at that one or two percent of the population who are looking for something special and are willing to go some distance to find it," he continued. "Let me give you four examples. First, there are scores of adults today who are looking for a chance to be involved in ministry to other people. They want to go to a church where they make a difference, and they live in all parts of the city. Our downtown location offers us the opportunity to develop a number and variety of outreach ministries that simply aren't available to the typical suburban congregation. In asking people to serve on church committees we give first priority to staffing these groups that carry out our ministry to downtown. Only after these are staffed do we begin the process of picking the people to serve.

"Second, we try to have the finest ministry of music in the city, and our downtown location enables us to attract those people who find excellent music to be an essential part of the worship experience. We attract those who seek the challenge of singing in a top flight choir. Third, we run a weekday Christian nursery school for two-, three-, and four-year-olds that is widely recognized among the professionals concerned with the development of the young child as the finest in this part of the state. There aren't enough parents who really want that quality to make it educationally and economically viable unless you have a convenient central location.

"Fourth, we try to offer people the chance to be with other people from all walks of life, all occupations and vocations, all age groups, all income levels, and all parts of the city, as they participate in the life and ministry of Central Church. Most of the housing, built here in the last thirty years, is segregated by age, income, occupation, color, and education. The church, located in a suburban residential community, is bound to reflect that thin slice of the total population spectrum. Our downtown location gives us a tremendous advantage in these and several other areas."

"Our biggest problem here at Briarwood Church is the turnover. Most of the people living out here really are only passing through," explained a member of that seventeen-year-old suburban church. "They buy out here because of the schools, the summer recreation program, and because in an inflationary era it's cheaper to buy than to rent. Three, four, or five years later they move. It makes it almost impossible to build any sense of fellowship within our congregation or to develop continuity of leadership or program in the church."

"Perhaps the one distinctive characteristic of this congregation," declared the pastor of the twenty-two-year-old congregation with a meeting place two blocks west of the Briarwood Church, "is the turnover of the population. One-half of the people living here today were not living in Briarwood five years ago. This has stimulated our evangelistic outreach, our program planning, and our leadership development in a way I have never experienced before in over twenty years in the ministry. In some ways the high rate of mobility is our greatest asset. It forces us to be constantly involved in going out and witnessing to people that Jesus Christ is Lord and Savior. It forces us to plan a wide variety of fellowship events so the newcomers and the old-timers can get to know one another as persons. This high mobility forces our classes and groups to be open and receptive not only to new people, but also to new ideas and new leadership.

"The rapid turnover of the membership has made a joke out of that cliché, 'But we've never done it that way before.' I think the high mobility of the population is one of the most important factors in keeping this an open, vibrant, vital, evangelistic, and people-oriented congregation. Without the stimulation of saying farewell to 150 to 200 adult members and welcoming that many new members every year, it would be very easy for us to turn into a very complacent fellowship of old friends growing old together while we're drifting along in a very comfortable rut."

These three pairs of illustrations describe one of the basic issues in any systematic and intentional effort in church planning. Do you begin the process by listing the problems or by describing the potentialities? To use an old cliché, Is the glass of water half full or half empty?

There is no question but that many of us find it easier, and often more enjoyable, to begin the planning process by identifying what we believe is wrong and by listing the problems. One of the reasons why we tend to find this to be an attractive approach is that it leads us into reviewing the past. Since we all are more familiar with the past than with the future, we find it easier to review the past and the problems inherited from the past rather than to speculate about the potentialities of the future. The older we are, the more we know of the past and the more uncertain we are about the future.

By definition, however, planning is a future-oriented effort based on the premise that just as God has given us the gift of this day, he will give us another new day tomorrow. To plan is an act of faith, to express our trust that God will give us a tomorrow. The question is not whether we should plan, but how do we go about it and the persepctive that we as Christians bring to the planning effort as we look to the future. The difference between a problem-oriented and a potentialities-oriented perspective may determine whether we plan for yesterday or for tomorrow.

These three pairs of contrasting responses to contemporary reality also illustrate the central theme of this chapter which is that the choice of the planning model to be used will have a tremendous impact on the outcome of that effort.

Many congregations are tempted to use a problem-based approach to planning. Among the normal outcomes of the use of that model are these.

1. It tends to produce a strong past orientation. After all, our problems have their origin in the past.

The use of a potentialities-based approach to planning also has a half dozen predictable outcomes.

1. It tends to produce a strong future-orientation. Whenever the conversation is focused on potentialities, that automatically causes most people to think in terms of the future.

101

2. It tends to encourage pessimism. A typcial part of the problem-based planning model is to build a list of problems. Whenever several people join together to build a list, they usually build a longer list than any one person would be able to produce individually. The result, "Golly, things are worse than I thought they were. I knew we had problems, but I didn't know we had that many!"

3. It tends to reinforce an emphasis on remedial approaches. Again, the emphasis on problems tends to cause people to think in terms of developing remedies for yesterday's illnesses rather than concentrating on new opportunities for ministry and outreach.

4. It tends to foster a preoccupation with liabilities. The emphasis on problems, on scapegoating, and on what is not happening tends to focus the people's attention on their liabilities and weaknesses.

5. It tends to encourage scapegoating. "We certainly do have a lot of problems here, and if you'll give me a minute, I'll explain why we have them. It wasn't our last minister, but the one before him who . . ."

2. It tends to enhance optimism. A typical part of any planning effort is to build a list. Whenever several people join together to create a list, they usually produce a list longer than any one person would have been able to create. The result, "Golly! I knew there was still some basis for hope left, but I never realized we had this many different opportunities still open to us!"

3. It tends to nurture creativity. Whenever people are encouraged to identify potentialities, to look toward the future, and to see new possibilities in ministry, that tends to stimulate creative thinking.

4. It tends to encourage people to identify, affirm, and build on assets as they look creatively at new potentialities and opportunites in ministry. Planning from strength causes people to identify strengths.

5. It tends to attract and motivate new adult members to become involved in the planning and the implementation of new ministries; new adult members usually have positive feelings about the congregation

which they just joined, or they would not have chosen to unite with it. While a problem-based approach to planning tends to exclude newcomers because of the past-orientation, and new members usually do not have any first-hand knowledge of that past or of the origins of today's problems, new members know as much about the future as anyone else and frequently are more enthusiastic about the future since they do not carry the baggage of the past.

6. It tends to produce frustration-stimulated goals in response to institutional needs. "We have all of that empty Sunday school space. Let's try to reach more children to fill up those empty rooms." Thus the goals tend to be generated by institutional maintenance pressures rather than in response to the needs of people.

6. It tends to encourage the formulation of goals in response to the unmet needs of people. For example, scores of downtown congregations have identified their location as an asset in seeking to minister to single parents. That raises the question, How do we develop a ministry to single adults? That question leads to another question, What are the needs of single parents that are not being met by other churches? Thus, programmatic goals tend to be developed in response to the needs of people rather than in response to institutional pressures to recreate yesterday or to fill empty rooms.

103

What Is the Level of Self-Esteem?

A second factor in choosing a planning model is to consider the impact of each alternative planning model on the morale or self-esteem of the congregation. Too often a planning model is chosen which causes the members to feel inadequate, overwhelmed by their problems, or depressed by a comparison of today's statistics with the enriched recollections of yesterday.

Perhaps the most subtle difference between a problem-based approach to church planning and a potentialities-based approach relates to the matter of congregational self-esteem. Whenever a congregation develops a complete list of the problems and obstacles before it, this is almost certain to produce a sense of inadequacy, helplessness, and low self-esteem. The dynamics of simply identifying and listing all the problems can be a very depressing experience, even for the more optimistic members of the group. Such an exercise is also vulnerable to the counterproductive diversions of scapegoating, second-guessing the past, and trying to live yesterday all over again.

By contrast, identifying and listing the potentialities in ministry tend to cause people to look to the future, to be conscious of the assets and strengths of the congregation, to become more aware of the number and variety of programs and ministries now functioning, to see these as foundation stones or building blocks for expanding the outreach of the church, to recognize new possibilities for ministry, to try to identify the people not being reached by any congregation, and to perceive the future as open rather than closed.

In contrast to the problem-based approach to planning which tends to lower the level of congregational self-esteem, the potentialities-based approach tends to raise the level of congregational self-esteem. This is a very crucial point since every person and every organization tends to build projections into the future on the perception of contemporary reality and on the level of self-esteem of that individual or organization. The higher the level of self-esteem, the greater the degree of willingness to venture forth into an unknown tomorrow. The congregation with a high level of self-esteem will undertake new ministries which an identical congregation with a low level of self-esteem would not even consider.[1]

Allocative or Creative?

The third factor to be considered in selecting a planning model is the most complex and involves a choice between two different beginning points.

In broad general terms, two sharply different planning styles have been developed in our society. The dominant style can be described as an *allocative* approach. It is based on the need to allocate scarce resources. A second style can be described as *innovative.* It is based on the assumption that planning should encourage the emergence of new ideas, creativity, and new solutions to problems.

Scores of models have been developed for the allocative approach. Perhaps 99 percent of the knowledge, skills, models, experiences, and theories in planning that accumulated in our culture have been for an allocative approach. As a result, almost all planning in our culture is allocative. This is most likely to be the case when the effort is directed by persons born before 1945 who were reared and trained in a society which concentrated all planning efforts under an allocative approach.

Every allocative planning model is based on the assumption that there is a scarcity of resources. Land use controls, such as zoning, assume a shortage of land and the need to allocate this scarce commodity among competing demands. Obviously, it has been much easier to sell the concept of zoning in New York City than in western Kansas or Texas or Oklahoma. The allocative approach requires a shortage, either real or artificial, of the resources on which the planning effort is focused. Today, for example, considerable frustration is being engendered by the use of traditional planning methods for the placement of veterinarians, teachers, surgeons, ministers, dentists, and lawyers because these placement systems were developed when there was a scarcity of such professionals; but there is now a surplus. By 1985 a similar frustration will be felt in the placement of managers and physicians as the supply begins to exceed the demand.

The allocative approach has dominated our society to the extent that people intuitively turn to an allocative model in a crisis. Thus, when the Arabs cut off the supply of petroleum to the U.S. in 1973, the national debate immediately focused on an allocative response. Some leaders urged the rationing of gasoline through the use of ration stamps. Others recommended a sharp increase in price. While this debate continued, the operational response was to ration gasoline by limiting the number of gallons per sale to the cars waiting in line, with their engines running and burning up gasoline at the local service station.

Unfortunately we have very limited experience with innovative approaches to planning. One of the few time-tested examples is in building codes. For many decades building codes were designed from an allocative approach and specified in detailed terms the materials that would be permitted in a construction project. Some codes even required the use of certain products specified by brand names. For the past three decades, however, the trend has been toward the development of building codes based on performance standards. This innovative approach has encouraged creativity by both the manufacturers of building materials and by the construction industry.

A more recent example is the shift from a cost-benefit model to a cost-effectiveness model in planning for the reduction of air and water pollution. An outstanding example of the use of an innovative approach is in Japan, where the central emphasis is not on allocating petroleum products but on replacing one source of cheap energy (petroleum) with another (hydrogen from sea water). One of the biggest contemporary disasters resulting from the use of an allocative approach can be found in the Occupational Safety and Health Administration rules, with its focus on detail rather than on encouraging innovative responses to the need for the greater safety and protection of health of people in an industrial society.

WHICH PLANNING MODEL?

The basic thesis of this chapter is that the choice of the planning model will have a major impact on the outcome of the planning effort. Therefore it follows, if the decision is made to emphasize creativity and innovation in the planning effort, the process should begin by choosing an innovative planning model. That is exactly right! It also is far more difficult than it sounds for two reasons.

The more complex of the two reasons is that the choice of the planning model to be used tends to be a product of the conceptual framework used to define the problem. Thus if the problem is defined in "shortage" terms, this naturally causes the participants to feel more comfortable with an allocative planning model. Even if an effort is made to begin with an innovative planning model, the way the problem has been defined soon causes the effort to drift over to a discussion of the allocation of scarce resources. After all, there are only twenty-four hours in a day, and 365 days in a year; therefore, any planning effort dealing with a time frame of any type inevitably must deal with the allocation of that finite commodity, time! Likewise, most planning efforts soon move to a consideration of such other finite resources as personnel, space, money, and materials.[2] This usually causes any effort that begins with an innovative planning model to move toward an allocative approach in order to ration what are perceived to be finite resources.

In other words, the terms that are used to define the nature of the problem and the conceptual bias of those defining the problem have a tremendous influence on the choice of a planning model!

As a result of what appears to be an inevitable tendency of normal human beings, who were reared in a world which has emphasized the scarcity of resources, to define most problems in terms that create a need for an allocative planning model, it may be that the most that can be expected is to encourage more planning efforts *to begin with an innovative model*. That will tend to encourage creativity and postpone the time when the rationing mentality takes over that planning effort. Eventually it may even lead to a different conceptual framework for defining the nature of that problem!

An excellent illustration of this today is to review the efforts in the United States in planning for the use of energy. This began with the definition of the problem as a shortage of gasoline following the

Arab embargo of 1973 and soon changed to an emphasis on a shortage of petroleum. Gradually the problem was redefined as a shortage of low-priced petroleum, next it was redefined as an "energy problem," soon thereafter it was redefined as a "shortage of cheap energy," and eventually it was redefined as a balance of payments problem. Each of these definitions fits an allocative approach to planning for the problem and therefore it is very easy to turn to that approach rather than seek an innovative planning model. Each of these definitions of the nature of the problem automatically leads into a rationing approach to problem-solving!

Some day, however, the nature of the problem will be defined, in different terms. There is not a shortage of sources of cheap energy. The world has a huge supply of free-for-the-taking energy in sunlight, in the winds, in the tides, and in the hydrogen in sea water. The problem is that we do not now have the technology to take the energy in the tides and turn it into low-priced electricity or to take the energy in the sunlight to heat homes in the northern states to a comfortable temperature in January or to extract the energy from sea water and put it in the gas tanks of automobiles. (It should be noted here that the Japanese have developed the technology to extract hydrogen from sea water and use it to power automobiles. They have found that internal combustion engines run better and cleaner on hydrogen than on gasoline, but the Japanese have yet to develop a distribution system for hydrogen equal to the distribution system for gasoline.)

Eventually the energy problem in the United States will be redefined, and innovative planning models will be used to discover the technology to use the energy from the sun to heat homes to comfortable standards[3] or to take the energy in sea water to power automobiles. An allocative planning model will be of limited help in responding to those definitions of the problem. When the problem is redefined from being perceived as a shortage of petroleum or as a balance of payments issue to a shortage of the technology necessary to shift from one source of cheap energy to another source of cheap energy, it will be much easier to persuade people to turn to innovative planning models.

The American tendency to define problems in terms that

encourage the use of allocative planning models is back of the second reason that it is difficult to encourage greater use of an innovative approach to planning. In simple terms, there is a shortage of innovative planning models. Most of the experience in planning in the North American continent has been concentrated in developing allocative planning models. This point can be illustrated by looking at a few examples of the two types of planning models.

ALLOCATIVE PLANNING MODELS	INNOVATIVE PLANNING MODELS
A materials-based building code	A performance-based building code
Problem-based planning	Potentialities-based planning
Budgeting	Policies planning
Cost-benefit planning	Affirm and build on strengths
Zoning	Cost-effectiveness planning
Nominating committees	Management by objective
Unified budgets	
Planning-budgeting-evaluation	
Zero-based budgeting	
Counting	
Ministerial placement systems	

It would be relatively easy to list another two dozen specific allocative planning models, but far more difficult to add another half dozen examples of innovative planning models. As was pointed out earlier, perhaps 99 percent of the knowledge, wisdom, skills, insights, and experience in planning has been concentrated in the development of allocative planning models. Very little has been done in expanding our knowledge and skills in innovative planning.

Five Implications

In summarizing what this says to church leaders it may be helpful to suggest five specific implications.

EFFECTIVE CHURCH PLANNING

First, resist the temptation to concentrate on weaknesses, problems, liabilities, and the past. While at times it will be necessary to deal with problems and weaknesses, a safe rule is always begin by identifying, affirming, and building on strengths.

Second, the quality of the self-image is always a very influential factor in how a congregation (or any organization or individual) evaluates its potential, identifies its assets and liabilities, and views the future. Therefore in a majority of cases, the beginning point in any planning effort should be to raise the level of self-esteem.

Third, threshing machines produce straw, and silo fillers produce silage. The choice of the planning approach to be used will have a greater impact on the recommendations coming out of that effort than any other single factor.

Fourth, the most effective means of encouraging creativity and a future-orientation in planning is to begin with an innovative planning model.

Finally, the way the problem or issue is defined will have a significant impact on the self-esteem of the people involved, the choice of a planning approach, the data to be gathered, and, therefore, the outcome of the entire process. One of the caution signs is to begin by identifying strengths, assets, resources, and potentialities rather than to begin by listing weaknesses, liabilities, problems, and shortcomings. Another caution sign is to distinguish between problems and symptoms, but that is the subject of the next chapter.

Symptoms or Problems?

"Here's our problem," explained John Erickson, chairman of the finance committee at Westminster Church. "Last year we dipped into our reserves to pay for a new roof, to resurface the parking lot, and to be able to pay the full amount we had budgeted for benevolences. That added up to a $50,000 deficit. We received $75,000 from member giving and spent a total of $125,000. This year it appears that member giving will be approximately $66,000, and we will have expenses of $84,000 if we pay the budgeted amount for benevolences. My guess is we can look forward to about $60,000 in member contributions for this coming year, but unless we make some additional major cuts, our expenses will be at least $80,000. That means three consecutive years of dipping into our reserves to balance out. If we keep this up, our reserves will be all gone in another three or four years. If we don't balance our budget pretty soon, we'll be moving from a problem to a crisis!"

"I don't see it quite the way you do, John," declared another member of the committee. "It seems to me our basic problem is the poor stewardship of our members. If everyone tithed, we would have plenty of money. The problem is that our members give to the church out of what they have left over, not out of the first tenth of their income."

"There's another dimension that you both have ignored," suggested a third member of the committee. "We've been a declining church ever since Reverend Lee resigned back in 1958. Reverend Duncan, who followed Lee, was a disaster, even though he only stayed four years, and we've not recovered. During the past twenty years our membership has dropped by half, and for the past four or five years our worship attendance has been decreasing at the rate of 5 or 6 percent per year. Our problem is that we have an expenditures budget of a 400-member church, but we're really only a 250-member congregation today."

What is the problem at Westminster?

"If you ask me, our problem is that we're too complacent," declared Tex Landis, a longtime member at Central Church. "Ever since we paid off the mortgage, we've been drifting. I'm sure you've all heard the old saying, 'Every church does its best when it has a mortgage.' I suggest we buy that house next door—it's for sale, you know—tear it down, and enlarge our parking lot."

"That's not our problem, Tex," objected another member from Central Church. "Our problem is we need a minister who can pull the people in and fill up our church. Last Sunday morning the church was half empty. Adding more parking won't fill the church. What we need is better preaching, not more parking."

"You're both wrong," retorted another longtime leader at Central. "The basic problem here is that our members aren't sufficiently committed. If they were more committed, we wouldn't have this complacency you refer to, Tex, and the church would be packed on Sunday morning, regardless of who was preaching."

"We've always been a family church," reflected Dave Fuller, a member of the pulpit search committee at the 450-member Hillside Church. "My wife and I joined this congregation in 1953, seven years after we were married. At that time Hillside was made up almost entirely of young married couples with small children. That was the focal point of our ministry and the source of our growth. If I remember correctly, around 1960 we had nearly 700 members on the rolls. During the last several years we seem to have lost some of our enthusiasm, and we're not reaching the young families like we used to be able to do. I think we should be looking for a dynamic young preacher with an attractive wife and a couple of kids, who can reach today's young families."

"You're right on target, Dave," agreed Billy Sewell, a fifty-one-year-old father of four and the next-to-youngest member of the committee. "What we need is more young families. That's the future for any church."

"I don't object to that," added Margaret Halvorson, "but let's not overlook the older members. Agnes and I went over the membership list name by name in preparation for this meeting, and let me tell you what we discovered. We have 74 members from families where there is a husband and wife living together and at least one child under eighteen years of age at home. That's 18 percent of 404 resident adult members. Again, in several cases either the husband or wife is not a member here at Hillside. All but nineteen persons in this group are at least forty-five years old. Those nineteen represent twelve couples who are still childless. Four of those young childless couples are almost completely inactive. Third, we have a total of 84 widowed persons in our membership. That's 21 percent of our resident adult membership."

"That's all very interesting, Margaret," interrupted Ray Thornton, "but what does all of this have to do with looking for a young minister who can rebuild this congregation around a strong family emphasis?"

"Please allow me to finish, and I'll explain why we went to all of this work and why I'm bringing this up," continued Margaret, "I brought along a summary sheet for each one of you which shows our membership distribution and compares it to the total American population." As she spoke, she handed out a sheet which contained this summary.

(See table on following page.)

"Now, if you look at the last line you'll see we have eight single-parent families with children under eighteen. All eight are divorced, six women and two men, and I have excluded them from the single adult category because they are really families. Finally, we have 32 single adults, in addition to the eight single parents, and they account for eight percent of our adult members. Most of them are young single adults, but thirteen are persons who are at least fifty years of age and either divorced or never married."

"Thank you, Margaret, for all of your work," exclaimed Dave

EFFECTIVE CHURCH PLANNING

FAMILY AND MARITAL STATUS
(Resident adult members age 18 and over)

Number		Hillside	USA
74	Husbands and wives living together with children under 18 at home	18%	34%
206	Husbands and wives without children under 18 at home	51%	31%
24	Single, never married adults	6%	18%
13	Currently divorced	3%	6%
3	Currently separated from spouse	1%	3%
84	Currently widowed	21%	8%

Fuller. "You've just documented my case. I didn't know the exact figures, but it's clear we're getting to be an old congregation, and we need a new minister who can help us rebuild this as a family church the way it was back in the fifties."

"You've completely missed my point, Dave!" replied Margaret. "The reason Agnes and I went to all this work was to prove to some of you dumb men that Hillside is a congregation of mature adults today, and we should be looking for a mature and experienced minister who can be an effective pastor to mature adults. Last year, for example, we lost thirteen members by death, and the year before it was eleven. That's double the denominational average for a church of our size. We're getting older, and we need a mature pastor who can minister to older members."

"I agree with your diagnosis, Margaret, but not with the prescription," argued Billy Sewell. "We are an old congregation, and we're getting older; therefore, if this congregation is to survive, we need a young minister who can reach young families."

What is the problem at Hillside Church?

"I'm afraid if we don't raise the minister's salary for the next year, we'll lose her," observed Al Otis as he met with three other members of the 78-member Oak Hill Church to prepare a recommendation on the minister's salary for the coming year.

"Well, I want to keep her," responded Mary Brenna, "but I don't see how we can afford to give her more than a token increase. Where will we get the money?"

"You may hate me for saying this," declared Linda Harper, "but I'm not sure but that I'm ready for her to leave. She has so many ideas and so much energy and is so persuasive that I'm getting worn out. I'm about ready for a six- or eight-month vacancy or for a retired minister who won't push so hard. All of her ideas are good ones, but I have a full-time job besides being a housewife and a mother, and I'm getting tired. She is the full-time pastor of a forty-five-family congregation and expects us to be able to keep up with her pace."

"Well, I don't want to see her leave," declared Linda's husband, Tom. "She's the best preacher and the most energetic and creative minister we've had in the twenty years I've been a member here, and I hate to think of the future if she moves on. We'll never be able to find a man to match her who would be willing to come here. Maybe we can get some help from the denomination in order to give her the salary increase she deserves. After all, why be a member of a denomination unless it's there to help when you need help?"

"I'm a little surprised at your comment, Linda, but I guess we're all tired," offered Al Otis. "She expects a lot of us and I admire her for that, but I know she is disappointed the church hasn't grown. I've tried to explain to her there just isn't much potential for growth out here in the country. We've been averaging between fifty and sixty at worship for at least fifteen years and for the last half-dozen ministers, so I doubt if there's any chance it will go up much. I'm surprised our attendance has held up as well as it has, considering that for years we used to have over a hundred members and now we're down to fewer than eighty."

"I agree with you, Al," added Mary Brennan. "I think we're dealing more with a question of morale than with money. She's been here three years now, and I believe she is getting a little discouraged that things haven't picked up more. Every preacher wants their church to grow. I'm afraid that if we don't raise her salary, she may feel we don't appreciate how hard she's been working and what a good job she's been doing. We simply have to find the money someplace to raise her salary!"

What is the problem at Oak Hill Church?

The Emphasis on Symptoms

These four conversations illustrate a widespread pattern that can be found in literally thousands of churches. The discussion wanders all around what appears to be the agenda item under consideration without ever being focused on a clearly defined central issue or problem or concern. Symptoms are identified and discussed, but the discussion never reaches the point of identifying the central issues. The participants identify a variety of aches, pains, hopes, fears, biases, concerns, and frustrations without ever getting to a diagnosis of the basic cause of those feelings. This distinction between symptoms and problems can be illustrated by going back and taking a second brief look at each of the conversations.

At Westminster the basic issue is not the annual deficit. That is only a symptom of a more basic problem, the lack of agreement on priorities. If the members could agree on the priorities for expenditures, it would be possible to develop a budget that would keep the anticipated expenditures within the amount of the anticipated receipts.

A slightly more complex definition of the basic issue would be to discover why the congregation has been engaged in deficit financing. To avoid making hard decisions? The lack of a responsible decision-making body that could make difficult decisions? Ignorance on the part of the leaders about the financial facts of life? Or is this an intentional effort to avoid cuts in program funds during what is seen as a transitional period between years of steady decline and a new era of prospective growth in outreach, ministry, and membership?

Instead of discussing purpose, program, and priorities, however, the participants in this discussion identified such symptoms as the size of the deficit, the level of giving of the members,[1] the fact that the membership total had declined much more rapidly than the level of expenditures, and an unhappy pastorate that ended nearly twenty years earlier.

At Central Church the leaders described such symptoms as complacency, apathy, an excessive dependence on a minister, the lack of commitment by the members, and the low worship attendance. Again these appear to be symptoms of a more basic issue which is the change in the nature of the goals. Apparently the people at Central once were united around the goal of a building program, and this was followed by the goal of paying off a mortgage. Now that those two specific, attainable, measurable, visible, satisfying, and unifying goals have been achieved, the congregation apparently has drifted into a goalless stance which frequently is accompanied by such symptoms as apathy, a low level of enthusiasm, declining participation, and a growing passivity by the laity who wait for the pastor to take the initiative in the formulation of new goals. A closely related problem is that it appears after years of training the lay leadership to feel competent in leading in the implementation of real estate and financial goals, no one has retrained the lay leaders to feel competent and self-confident in formulating and implementing ministry goals.

At the aging Hillside congregation the members identified such symptoms as the fact that the members are growing older (a normal phenomenon, all lucky people grow older with every passing day), the decline in the membership total, a shift from a congregation composed largely of younger two-generation households to a congregation composed largely of one-generation households, a widespread desire to turn the calendar back a quarter of a century, again an excessive dependence on finding a pastor who, hopefully, will reverse the trend, a comparatively high death rate, institutional survival concerns, and the implication that the life cycle of a congregation parallels the life cycle of a human being.

Margaret Halvorson came fairly close to identifying one of the basic issues: should the congregation place the high priority on seeking to reach young families as replacement members or on a ministry to mature adults? Margaret, however, concentrated her

117

comments on the descriptive statistical analysis she had made of the family and marital status of the adult membership and never fully communicated the basic conflict in priorities that is the heart of the issue at Hillside. Do these people believe God is calling Hillside Church to reach and attract young families in order to continue this congregation for another two or three decades? Or do they believe God is calling Hillside to maintain a ministry to mature adults? Or what is God calling Hillside Church to be and to do in this part of the twentieth century? That is the basic issue, but it was largely concealed by several layers of symptoms and statistics.

The discussion among the four leaders at the 78-member Oak Hill Church also identified a variety of symptoms and means-to-an-end issues, but almost completely ignored the more basic questions. Among the symptoms that were described were the financial squeeze that made questionable an increase in the salary of the minister for the coming year, the feeling that the congregation was overworked by this young and energetic pastor, again the belief that the future of the congregation might rest on the minister (although this congregation apparently had remained very stable in worship attendance through the tenure of several pastors), a reluctance to have to face another change in pastoral leadership, a question about the role of the denomination and the reason for a denominational affiliation, the concern over the morale of the minister, and the need to find some more money someplace.

While Linda Harper almost brought it up, this group of four leaders never really asked the basic question of, "Do we need, can we justify, and can we afford a full-time pastor for a 78-member congregation?" The issue may not be of too little money, it may be too much pastor for too few people. The pastor may be suffering more from being under employed rather than from being under paid or under appreciated, but the basic purpose of the Christian Church is not providing employment and satisfactions for clergy. While these concerns represent a commendable attitude on the part of these four members, they obscure the more basic stewardship questions about the deployment of ministers and the porportion of the total receipts of a congregation that can be allocated to the financial support of a minister.

Influencing the Response

These four brief case studies also illustrate how the definition of the problem influences the choice of a planning model for developing a response to that issue. In the first case, for example, the leaders at Westminster Church were focusing their discussion on a budget deficit rather than talking purpose and priorities. This beginning point almost automatically will lead them into some form of rationing or allocative planning model as they respond to the variety of problems that usually emerge with the long-term decline in size of a congregation when that is accompanied by a budget deficit.

At Central Church the search for a scapegoat was already well underway. While one member nominated the minister and another nominated the members, it does not appear that this will be a very productive process for launching a new and exciting chapter in ministry and outreach. Instead of using this problem-based planning model, it probably would be better to use one of these four possibilities.

One alternative would be to launch a congregation-wide series of Bible study groups which would explore the New Testament definition of the church. On this foundation could be built a

Purpose ◊ Program ◊ Operational Goals ◊ Evaluation

model which would begin with a definition of the purpose and role of Central Church today and tomorrow, a description of the program necessary to fulfill that purpose, a formulation of the specific, attainable, and measurable operational goals necessary for developing that program and a system of evaluation, including a time frame with mileposts, for subsequent evaluation of the progress made in implementing those goals.

A second alternative would be to use a potentialities-based planning model and begin by identifying the assets they had in their debt-free meeting place, the advantages of that location, the strengths of the program, the major competencies of the staff, the

119

gifts and talents of the lay leadership, and their other resources. After this had been completed, they could begin to identify the needs of unchurched people which were not being met by other worshiping congregations in the city and discover where their strengths and resources matched an unmet need.

A third alternative would be to move into a systematic goal-setting process using management-by-objective techniques.

A fourth alternative would be to begin to dream about the future and seek to identiy what God is calling Central Church to be and to be doing five years hence. After this has been done, they could identify contemporary reality at Central, and this would lift up the discrepancy between the vision of five years hence and the reality of today. This discrepancy could be the basis for moving into a goal-setting process.

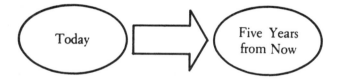

The planning effort would be focused on getting from here (the reality of today) to there (the vision of what God is calling Central Church to be and to be doing five years hence).

The chances for a productive outcome would be enhanced if the effort was accompanied by a program for retraining the leadership, who apparently had had years of experience in implementing real estate and finance goals, to improve their competence in setting and implementing ministry goals.[2]

The one planning model which should be avoided at Central Church would be the widely used church and community study in which an analysis is made of the congregation and its property and that is accompanied by a study of the neighborhood surrounding the meeting place. This planning model usually produces recommendations on real estate and finances. The probability of this happening at Central Church would be enhanced by the leaders' long experience in working with real estate and finance issues. Central Church should choose a planning model which will produce recommendations on ministry and outreach rather than encourage a continued emphasis on land and money.

The leaders at the Hillside Church with its aging membership were defining their situation in a manner that would encourage them to use a problem-based planning model (see pages 112-114). This would reinforce the past-orientation, emphasize a remedial rather than a creative approach to contemporary reality, encourage scapegoating, place a high priority on frustration-stimulated goals formulated in response to institutional survival pressures, rather than the needs of unchurched people, and feed the fires of pessimism. A far more creative approach would be to begin by evaluating the assets, strengths, resources, and potentialities for ministering to that rapidly growing number of mature adults in the population. This could produce a far stronger future-orientation in the planning effort and also encourage the formulation of goals developed on the basis of the strengths of this congregation and in response to the needs of unchurched mature adults.

At the rural Oak Hill Church, the kindly and somewhat paternalistic leaders had drifted into a discussion which was making a means-to-an-end question, the satisfactions and financial compensation of the minister, into a basic goal in itself. While their concern for an adequate salary and for the personal satisfactions for their pastor is commendable, that is still a means-to-an-end issue. A better and more creative approach might be to begin by attempting to redefine the purpose and distinctive role of Oak Hill Church, developing the programmatic and ministry goals necessary for fulfilling that role and then looking at the means-to-an-end resources, such as staff, real estate, lay training programs, finances and lay leadership, necessary for implementing those goals. They might have discovered they did not need a full-time minister and should not allocate such a large proportion of their financial resources for the compensation of a paid staff person.

These four case studies are drawn from real life. They are used here to illustrate how easy it is to focus the discussion on symptoms rather than basic underlying issues, the prescription probably will be directed toward relieving the surface aches and pain rather than treating the basic problem. At times this can be a very complex process as is illustrated by the diagnosis of the many reasons why Mary Hunter is unhappy.

5

Why Is Mary Hunter Unhappy?

As Ted and Mary Hunter drove home from church last Sunday, Mary broke the silence by bursting out, "Ted, let's transfer our membership. I'm getting fed up with things at First Church! Let's transfer to a smaller congregation nearer home. I think we'd both be happier." As he listened, Ted Hunter silently wondered what he should say. He had known for some time that Mary was less than completely happy at First Church, but he was sure the cause was not that they lived six miles from First Church. "Why is Mary unhappy?" he wondered.

Ted and Mary had moved here from another state nine years ago last April. They had visited First Church the Sunday after they arrived, on the recommendation of their former pastor. When they had gone to pick up their fourth-grade daughter after Sunday school, they became involved in a conversation concerning the replacement of the fourth-grade teacher. The previous Thursday, her husband had been notified that he was being transferred, and the family would be moving three weeks hence. By the time they left church that first Sunday, Mary had agreed to be the temporary, replacement teacher for the fourth-grade class. She had taught the third- and fourth-grade class off and on for twenty years in the 205-member church they had just left. When the people at First Church discovered this, they had eagerly pressed her to serve as the temporary replacement, and Mary agreed to come and assist the present teacher for the next two Sundays. On the third Sunday she would have the complete responsibility for the class.

Three weeks later, Ted and Mary were received by letter of transfer into the membership of First Church. Five months later

Ted, who was an accountant, was asked to complete the unexpired term of the church treasurer who had moved out of town to take a new job.

Now, nine years later, at fifty-five years of age, Ted was still the treasurer of First Church, and Mary had become the permanent replacement teacher in the fourth-grade room.

The oldest child had gone off to college a year after the Hunters moved here. He was now married and the father of two children. The second child also had graduated from college and was married with one child. The third child, a daughter, married two years ago and moved back east with her husband. The fourth child, and third son, had dropped out of college halfway through his first year and was now employed as a motorcycle mechanic. The fifth child, their little girl of nine years ago, was completing her first year at college 375 miles away.

Every Sunday morning, week after week for nine years, Ted and Mary had left their house at 9:15 A.M. to drive to First Church. Mary liked to be at least fifteen minutes early for her class which began at 9:45. Ted went into the church office and helped count and package the offering from the 8:30 worship service and to take care of any accumulated paperwork. At 10:58 he met Mary in the corridor, and together they went to the 11:00 worship service. After worship, Mary usually returned to the fourth-grade room to straighten up and get a few things ready for the following Sunday, while Ted went to the office and helped to count and package the offering from the second service and to prepare the deposit slip for the bank.

Last Sunday as they approached the street leading to their home, Mary continued to urge that they give serious consideration to transferring their church membership to another congregation.

Why is Mary Hunter unhappy? Why does this fifty-three-year-old woman want to leave First Church?

Three Answers?

Mary's pastor, Jim Martin, knew that Mary had been growing increasingly unhappy in recent months, and he thought he knew the reason. Jim had been the senior minister at First Church for fifteen years, and he knew his flock. "It's the empty-nest syndrome," he said to himself as he drove away from a visit with the Hunters a few weeks earlier. "For twenty-eight years Mary had built a large share of her life around rearing those five children, and now the youngest one has flown the nest. Mary not only is lonely, she also feels obsolete, useless, and irrelevant. After being an essential part of the home for twenty-eight years, she naturally experiences a psychological letdown when the last of the five children leaves home. Here's a woman with a master's degree in English literature who had taught in high school for several years, began to raise a family, and spent the next twenty years concentrating on being a mother and a homemaker. Now that task has been completed, and she no longer feels needed. She needs a new challenge."

The part-time, semiretired minister of visitation at First Church, who was asked to preach only once or twice a year, also recognized that Mary was becoming increasingly despondent. "I don't know why," he said to himself one day, "but apparently Mary's commitment to Jesus Christ as Lord and Savior isn't as strong as it once was. My hunch is that she isn't getting the spiritual nourishment from the sermons that she received in her previous church. Maybe what this church needs to help Mary, and a lot of others, is better biblical preaching Sunday after Sunday and perhaps a week-long revival."

The twenty-nine-year-old minister of education at First Church had a different theory. Last week at the meeting of a special committee to review the volunteer staff needs in the Sunday school, Mary's name had come up. Betty Mackey had asked, "I wonder if we should offer Mary Hunter at least a year off. She's been teaching the fourth-grade class for at least seven or eight years now. When our Laura was in fourth grade, she really enjoyed Mary's class, but two years ago our Jimmy was bored all year, and this year Larry, our youngest, is in Mary's class and he hates it." Lois Wilson immediately came to Mary's support. "All three of our girls have gone through Mary's fourth-grade class. All three enjoyed it, and Becky says she remembers more of what she learned in Mary's class than in any other class she's been in, and she's now a sophomore in high school."

"I haven't heard any complaints," commented Craig Busby, "but if she's been teaching that long, maybe she deserves a sabbatical."

"That's exactly what I had in mind," quickly suggested the minister of education. "Mary is obviously not as happy and cheerful as she was when I came here six years ago. I believe she's tired. She needs a change. I believe we ought to have a policy that requires anyone who has taught for seven years or more to take a year off from teaching. I am convinced a year's sabbatical would do a lot for Mary's morale, her attitude, and whatever else may be wrong with her."

Now, what do you think is wrong with Mary Hunter?

Another Perspective

One approach to this question is to shift the focus away from Mary Hunter and to look at the larger context. The easiest way to be free to look at the context, rather than to focus on Mary, is to assume there is nothing wrong with Mary. The "problem" is not with Mary Hunter. The "problem" is what First Church is doing, and not doing, that causes Mary to be unhappy. There are least four major factors here that deserve careful consideration.

Perhaps the best place to begin is to look at the way new members are assimilated at First Church. In this congregation, as in many others, most new members fall into one of four categories: (1) they become part of a small group such as an adult Sunday school class or a prayer group or a men's club or a group within the women's organization, (2) they accept a role such as a Sunday school teacher, which helps them identify with this congregation, (3) they become involved in a meaningful task such as helping to count the offering or paint the parsonage or prepare the annual church dinner, or (4) they become inactive. Mary had been assimilated by virtue of her role as a teacher and Ted by his role as church treasurer and by the weekly task of helping to count and package the weekly offering.

The Fellowship Circle

There is another part of this assimilation process, however, which requires attention here. Most congregations can be

described by the use of two circles. The larger circle includes all the members. The smaller fellowship circle includes those members who "really feel a part of this congregation." The "rules" for admission into the fellowship circle vary from congregation to congregation and from time to time. At First Church, neither Ted nor Mary is inside the fellowship circle. Ted does not care. He is more object-oriented than person-oriented, and he has no real interest in being a part of the inner circle. He has a meaningful task and a compatible role, which together offer him all the satisfactions and psychic rewards he craves.

Mary, however, knows she is not inside the fellowship circle, and she is increasingly unhappy about it. She had assumed that in a large congregation, such as First Church, admission into the fellowship circle was earned by "works." She had been faithful and obedient. She had worked very hard in the Sunday school for nine years without complaining, and she did not feel that she was any closer to being included in the fellowship circle at First Church than she was eight years ago!

Unfortunately, no one had ever told Mary that the "rules" at First Church laid out four easy routes into the fellowship circle: (a) by active participation in one of the five adult Sunday school classes, (b) by inheritance from parents who had been in the fellowship circle a generation earlier, (c) by the combination of long service on the Board and a gregarious personality, and (d) by being a part of one or more of the many small groups which together constitute the larger fellowship circle at First Church: various Bible study and prayer groups, the church bowling league, the Men's Brotherhood, the women's organization, the adult Sunday school classes, and several of the standing committees. Only the extroverted, highly sociable, and gregarious newcomers entered the fellowship circle at First Church by works. Typically they represent about 3 percent of the total church population, and quiet Mary is not a part of that 3 percent.

The Support System

A second reason that Mary Hunter is unhappy concerns the support system for teachers and other leaders in the church. Until they had joined the 1400-member First Church, neither Ted nor Mary had ever been members of a congregation with more than 250 members. In most smaller congregations there is a highly informal, but very effective, support system for every teacher and leader. The small congregation intuitively "looks after" the personal, spiritual, morale, and family needs of every teacher and leader in a very informal but extremely sensitive and supportive manner.[1] This ad hoc support system rarely functions automatically in the large congregation. First Church is no exception to this pattern, and since no one has created a support system for the teachers in the children's department, there was a high turnover among the teachers.

The two exceptions to this high turnover rate were Mary, who stuck it out because of personal perseverance, and the four women who had combined the fifth- and sixth-grade classes into one large class, which they taught as a team in the room next to where Mary's fourth-grade class met. There, Lois Frost, Joan Roswell, Carol McFee, and Agnes Peterson had created their own mutual support group. Together, with the occasional help of husband or teen-age son or daughter, these four women taught as a team. The high morale of the teachers, the enthusiasm of the fifth- and sixth-graders, and the record attendance made that class the envy of the whole Sunday school—but, it also obscured the need for a support system for teachers such as Mary Hunter, who taught alone.

It also meant that every Sunday morning Mary saw these four happy teachers come together in the room next door. As she heard them talking, laughing, and obviously enjoying themselves, Mary asked herself, "What's wrong with me? Why are they getting so much satisfaction out of teaching Sunday school, and I'm finding it less of a challenge and more of a chore every year?"

Silver Beavers and Dead Rats

Last April two members of the largest adult class at First Church came to the Senior Minister and asked permission to give an award to the couple who had served as co-presidents of the class for nearly two years and were about to move to Houston. The pastor agreed and on the following Sunday morning this couple was asked to come to the chancel at the 11 o'clock service. On behalf of the adult class, two representatives from that group came up and presented them with an engraved silver tray as a token of the gratitude the members felt for their volunteer efforts and wished them Godspeed on their journey to a new home.

As they drove home from church that same Sunday last April, Ted said, "Mary, if I remember correctly, today is the ninth anniversary of your teaching fourth grade here in the Sunday school." "No," replied Mary, "last Sunday was my ninth anniversary."

This incident illustrates two points that bear on Mary's unhappiness. First, every congregation has some system for handing out thank-yous or words of appreciation (silver beavers) to lay volunteers. Most congregations also are proficient at overlooking or criticising other lay volunteers and rewarding their efforts with criticism or total neglect or scornful comments (dead rats).[2] First Church thanked one couple for two years of service as co-presidents of an adult class by presenting them with a silver tray in a highly visible ceremony, and completely ignored Mary's ninth anniversary as the teacher of the fourth-grade class. Even Ted, her husband, handed her a dead rat by not remembering the correct anniversary date.

The second element illustrated by this incident is that in most congregations the internal reward system recognizes and expresses appreciation for the work of lay volunteers with adults, with youth, and with the administrative apparatus of the church. Persons who work with children, however, usually have very low visibility, tend to be overlooked, and are more likely to be awarded dead rats ("Why don't they teach the kids more Bible?" or "Why does she let those kids run in the halls?") rather than silver beavers.

A third reason Mary Hunter is unhappy is that she had collected several dead rats, but no silver beavers for her nine years of faithful service.

Visual and Verbal Skills

A fourth, and the most complex reason for Mary's unhappiness has two major facets to it. They are interrelated, but it may be best to discuss them separately in order to clarify the diagnosis and simplify suggesting a prescription.

One facet of this fourth reason for Mary's unhappiness grows out of a major shift in our society. Mary, like most of the others of her generation, was reared in a culture that emphasized competence in verbal skills. After graduating from college, Mary had gone to the state university for a master's degree in English literature and was teaching in a junior high school when she met Ted Hunter. She had continued to teach after marriage until about six months before their first child was born. By both natural gifts and formal education, Mary was a very verbal person. She enjoyed reading and had written several short stories, two of which had been published, and she would score very high on any test of verbal skills. Her God-given talents, training, experiences, and the era in which she was reared, all combined to reinforce her natural inclination to communicate verbally.

When she began teaching English literature to junior high school students back in the middle 1940s, she was working with people who had been born in the pre-television era of the 1930s when the culture in general, and radio in particular, emphasized the verbal channel of communication.

Now, however, as a fourth-grade teacher in the Sunday church school, Mary is working with children who were born into a world that increasingly emphasizes the use of nonverbal, visual channels in communication. Today's fourth-grader was born into a world in which television dominates the communication processes; a world in which remarkable progress has been achieved in developing educational techniques which utilize nonverbal, visual communication; and where there is more emphasis on learning by doing than learning by listening.

As the years passed, Mary continued to focus on verbal skills in her teaching methods and techniques. This was only natural; this was the way she had been taught. As the years passed, an increasing proportion of children in Mary's fourth-grade class became restless, bored, and frustrated. This, too, was only natural; these children have been reared in what is increasingly a visual-skill culture.

Most of Mary's problems were with fourth-grade boys who presented frustrating behavior problems for Mary. (A larger proportion of boys are naturally predominantly visual-skills-oriented than are girls—one reason why most of the children taking remedial reading courses are boys.) Two years ago there was David! One of the happiest days in Mary's life was the Sunday when, on the way home, she said to her husband, "Ted, I really feel like celebrating! Today is the last day I have to put up with David. That boy is the most disruptive force I have ever seen! The only cloud in the sky today is that I feel sorry for those teachers across the hall, who will have to put up with him for the next two years! But, there are four teachers over there, so they should be able to survive more easily than I did."

The next year it was the twins. Those boys were able to think of more ways to disrupt a class than anyone could imagine. On at least a dozen occasions Mary had felt like resigning, and on three different Sundays she had ordered the twins out of the classroom for the rest of the morning. As she reflected on these boys, Mary became a little more uneasy. She had felt sorry for those four teachers who were getting David when he was promoted to fifth grade. After a few weeks, however, she noticed that David was coming early and staying late for the fifth- and sixth-grade class. One Sunday she saw him walking in just ahead of her and called out, "David, how do you like Sunday school this year?" "It's the greatest!" he called back over his shoulder as he went roaring down the hall to his room.

When the twins moved to the fifth- and sixth-grade class, Mary was torn between relief and her neighbor-centered love for the four teachers across the hall who taught that class. Three months later at the monthly Sunday all-church family night and dinner the program included two presentations by the fifth- and sixth-grade Sunday school class. The first was a seven-minute, eight-millimeter "Documentary" on the burning of Rome and the church going underground, complete with sound on tape cassette. Mary was amazed to note that in the credits, David was listed as the "cinematographer," and the twins were listed as the "audio technicians." The second presentation was a series of color slides, also with sound on tape, depicting the life of Martin Luther. The fifth- and sixth-graders played the roles of various individuals in this sequence. Mary noted with interest that David was the star (he played Martin Luther). The twins were listed in the credits as responsible for historical background and sets.

As she sat and watched the remainder of the program that evening, Mary began to wonder, "Did those boys change that much when they moved into fifth grade, or was there something wrong in the way I tried to teach them?" Her self-doubts were not relaxed when, on the way out that evening, one of the twins came racing up to her and exclaimed, "Hullo, Mrs. Hunter. You oughta take a day off some Sunday and come over and visit our class. We're having a ball!"

Ten days later Mary happened to encounter the mother of the twins in the supermarket. As they chatted briefly Mary asked about the twins. "Oh, they're doing fine. The only problem we have is that for the past several months they've been getting us up so early every Sunday morning. They're afraid they'll be late for Sunday school and insist we get there early. Don't misunderstand me,

Mary, they really got a lot out of your class, but I guess they've matured more in the past few months, and now they really look forward to Sunday school in the way they never did before." As the two women parted company, Mary had another dead rat in her shopping cart.

Gradually Mary Hunter was accumulating a growing collection of dead rats as a verbal skill-oriented teacher trying to work with a generation of increasingly visual skill-oriented children. When the visual skill-oriented children moved from Mary's class to the fifth- and sixth-grade room, they entered a class where the pedagogical system was heavily oriented toward visual skill communication. The use of slides and movies and the writing of scripts caused the children who were primariy visual-skill-oriented to be far more interested in what was being taught.

Left-Brained and Right-Brained

Before moving to a discussion of the alternatives open to First Church and to Mary, it may help to look at the second facet of what has been happening to enable us to understand more clearly the verbal-visual distinction that was a major factor in Mary's increasing unhappiness.

Perhaps the best way to introduce this subject, which is the significance of the difference between the left hemisphere of the brain and the right hemisphere, is to refer to three sets of experiments.

The first concerns a phenomenon that was discovered when Dr. Robert Thorndike of the Teachers' College of Columbia University and his associates began to revise the standard IQ test. They discovered that the children born in the 1960s and the early 1970s had a higher than average IQ. Instead of the average child's IQ being 100, as it was for several decades, today's average two-year-old has an IQ of nearly 110, and this held true for three-year-olds, four-year-olds, and five-year-olds. At about age five and a half the average child's IQ began to decline until by age nine it was down to 101.

Why did these preschoolers test so high on IQ tests? The basic reason is these higher scores were primarily a result of the children doing better on the *nonverbal and visual* questions on the test than earlier generations of children had done on those type of questions.

Another experiment, conducted by Dr. Gerald Symes of the National Institute for Mental Health, discovered that third-grade boys with reading difficulties had above average capability for three-dimensional perception. The higher their level of competence for three-dimensional visualization, the more difficulty they had in reading.

Vadim Lvovich Deglin, the Russian neurophysiologist, has described the functional asymmetry of the brain as simply that one hemisphere has one set of specialized tasks and functions and the other hemisphere has another set of complementary tasks and functions. Deglin points out that while the left hemisphere of the brain has the faculty of speech, the ability to identify tones of voice, to distinguish between male and female voices, and to recognize musical tunes are primarily right hemisphere functions.[3] The left hemisphere of the brain, Deglin claims, controls logical and abstract thinking, while the right hemisphere governs concrete and imaginal thinking.[4]

Now what does all of this have to do wih Mary Hunter being unhappy?

As far as we can tell, Mary Hunter was and is by nature a predominantly left-brained, verbal skill-oriented person who grew up in a culture that taught people the way to succeed was to master the verbal skills of reading and writing. Her natural verbal skill-orientation was reinforced by her formal academic training, including the master's degree in English literature and teaching high school in the late 1940s.

When Mary began teaching a third- and fourth-grade Sunday school class in 1949, less than 3 percent of all homes in the nation had television sets. Today only 3 percent do *not* have a television set. In thirty years the cultural emphasis in communication had been changed radically by television. The fourth-grader of 1955 had grown to that age in the pre-television era when the basic cultural emphasis was on verbal communication. Today's fourth-grader was born into a world which has increasingly emphasized visual communication. One result is that the four-year-old of the 1970s does exceptionally well on the nonverbal visual questions on an IQ test.

Another result is that perhaps one-third or more of all boys have been encouraged to develop their natural right-brained visual communication skills but have not been forced to develop their left hemisphere verbal communication skills. Therefore when Mary said, "Now, children, let's gather in a circle and read our story," they were bored. Being bored, they became disruptive forces. When these same boys moved into the fifth- and sixth-grade classroom where the learning process rewarded competence in being able to conceptualize a three-dimension scene and write a script for it or arrange it to be photographed or to photograph it, they enjoyed participating. They were doing that which challenged their greatest competence.

Another result is that with each passing year the predominantly left-brained, verbal-skilled Mary Hunter became more and more out of step with the new generation of fourth-graders who were increasingly visual skill-oriented. The English-speaking person feels at home in a neighborhood where everyone speaks English. However, if as time passes and the English-speaking people move away and are replaced by Latvian- or Russian- or Spanish- or Korean- or French-speaking newcomers, eventually the one remaining English-speaking resident will begin to feel frustrated and unhappy. That is how the predominantly verbal skill-oriented Mary Hunter began to feel as more and more of the fourth graders coming to her class were children who had been encouraged to develop their right-hemisphere competence in visual communication.

Planning a Response

How should the people at First Church respond to Mary Hunter?

There are several obvious responses. In a large congregation,

Sunday school teachers should be encouraged to teach in teams or provided with a support system. Someone should have taken the responsibility to make sure that Mary received more silver beavers. Possibly she should have been encouraged to take a year off after teaching her first year or two. Whoever is responsible for membership care at First Church should have encouraged Ted and Mary to become active members of one of the small groups or to join an adult Sunday school class, even if this would have meant finding someone else to teach the fourth-grade class. Teachers need to be nurtured. Their spiritual and personal growth is important! These are among the more obvious responses to Mary's increasing unhappiness. To some extent, they could be preventive actions, and to some extent these are responses to symptoms.

Two other possible responses also merit consideration. The first is the more subtle. As the people at First Church gradually became aware of Mary's increasing unhappiness, they followed the normal and predictable pattern of asking, "What's wrong with Mary?" A better response would have been to ask, "What are we doing, or not doing, as a congregation that causes this faithful and dedicated Sunday school teacher to become so unhappy that she wants to leave this church?" This type of question usually will produce a different diagnosis than one which is focused on what is wrong with Mary.

Second, and closely related to that issue is the matching of a lay volunteer with a need. Mary began teaching fourth grade as a result of a sudden vacancy when the previous teacher's husband was transferred out of town. Mary was an experienced teacher and was available to fill an unexpected vacany. Nine years later she was still filling that vacancy.

A different method of placing lay volunteers in the church is to shift the focus from the needs of the institution to the gifts, talents, and strengths of the individual. It is possible that Mary, with her earlier experience teaching English literature in high school, would have been a very effective teacher for an adult class filled with verbal skill-oriented people born during the first three or four decades of this century. Mary might have found that class to be a very satisfying and rewarding experience. The class could have served as a support group for Mary and undoubtedly would have been generous in giving her silver beavers.

In some churches it is necessary to find people to "fill the holes." If this was the case at First Church, some attention could have been given to the continuing education of Mary to help this predominantly left-brained, verbal skill-oriented teacher understand the societal change that has been occurring and to help her improve her skills in teaching visual-skill-oriented fourth-graders. In other words, First Church might have made a greater effort to find a compatible group of people for Mary to teach, or they could have helped her understand why a predominantly left-brained adult may have difficulty communicating with some predominantly right-brained fourth-grade boys. That would have been better than focusing on "What's wrong with Mary?" The churches already have a high level of competence in making people feel guilty, but that is the subject of the next chapter.

6

Guilt, Morale, and Motivation

"We must have four more Sunday school teachers by the first of the month or we may not be able to offer any classes for junior high or senior high youth," threatened the pastor during the announcement period as he looked out over the crowd of two hundred people who had gathered to worship God that Sunday morning. "If any one of you feels called by God to help out in this crisis, please see me or the Sunday school superintendent after the service. This is the third Sunday in a row that I've been forced to make this announcement," continued the pastor, "and thus far not one of you has responded. I guess I'll just have to keep on begging until four of you volunteer to honor the commitment you made when you united with this congregation."

"We're asking everyone in the women's organization to shift to a new circle for this next year," announced the president of that group at Main Street Church to the other members of the executive committee. "This will enable every one of us to meet more people, make new friends, and share in new experiences."

"This is only a temporary arrangement," explained the chairman of the building committee at Zion Church to the members at a congregational meeting in 1960. "Last fall we all agreed we must relocate, although we knew this would mean some temporary inconvenience. Our proposed plans call for construction of a fellowship hall, which we will use as our temporary place

139

for worship, plus six classrooms, offices, and restrooms. This means we'll have to have two worship services for several years, because of the limited space, but we expect that we'll be able to construct the permanent sanctuary by the early 1970s."

Fifteen years after the completion of this construction program that same man remarked, "Somehow I feel we have failed! When we relocated to this site, I felt absolutely certain that we would have the new sanctuary up by now, but we haven't been able to do it. Our projections on growth turned out to be way too high, building costs have skyrocketed, and we have had three different pastors since we moved out here. I'm sixty-three years old now, and I still feel we must keep the commitment we made to our people back in 1960, but our new minister wants to remodel the fellowship hall into a permanent sanctuary. I know we can't afford to build right now, but if we go ahead with the remodeling, I'm afraid our people will become so satisfied with the arrangement that we'll never be able to complete our master plan. I just know that if we could build a big new sanctuary, as we planned to do back in 1960, our congregation would grow."

"I don't know why it is, but our members simply won't sit in those front pews," observed an usher at Bethel Church. "We've tried to rope off the back pews, the minister has pleaded with the people, and we've tried everything we can, but they refuse to sit in those front pews. Every Sunday I try to usher some of the first arrivals down to the front pews, but they just shake their heads and slip into one of the back pews."

"We emphasize family worship here at Trinity," declared an influential layman of that 585-member congregation. "We strongly encourage parents and children to sit together in the same pew at worship. We do have a few problems implementing that policy because some of the kids insist on sitting with their friends, rather than with their parents, but we do discourage that."

"Every church should have as its first priority ministering to the people living in the community around that congregation's meeting place," proclaimed a denominational executive at a regional meeting of lay leaders from three dozen congregations. "When you evaluate your church's ministry, the first question you should ask yourself is, What are we doing to reach out to the people living around your church? That should be the beginning point for evaluating your evangelistic outreach."

What do these half-dozen incidents have in common? What is the common thread running through all six? What relevance do they have in a book on church planning?

All six illustrate one of the neglected factors in church planning that often has serious consequences. This is the excessive use of guilt in planning and administration. Or, to state it in more precise terms, all six incidents illustrate one of the skills many churches have developed to a remarkably high level of competence. This is the skill to make people feel guilty about being normal!

Many of the clichés one hears in the churches, much of the conventional wisdom that influences church planning, and most of the frustrations that aggravate church leaders tend to induce a feeling of guilt when results are compared to dreams of how it should be.

What Is the Point?

Before looking in more detail at several common examples of this pattern, it may be helpful to articulate the two basic assumptions on which this chapter is based. First, most of us have the ability to respond creatively to normal patterns of behavior. By contrast, we usually find it far more difficult to respond creatively to what we perceive as abnormal behavior. The basic problem, however, is not in the behavior patterns of individuals and institutions. The heart of the problem is in our tendency to confuse how things are with how we believe "it should be here." We tend to mislabel normal and predictable behavior patterns as "bad" and to cause people, sometimes ourselves and sometimes others, to feel guilty about what is in fact normal and predictable behavior

141

patterns. Too often we act as though we believe that God's will can prevail only if our side wins and if people do what we believe they should do. This attitude is difficult to reconcile with a doctrine of sin.

A simple example of this is the common tendency of the first-born child in the family, who typically is comparatively serious, achievement-oriented, persistent, conscientious, in need of peer group approval, "successful," and responsible, to place unrealistic expectations on the younger brother or sister. The typical middle-born child tends to be more sociable, less task-oriented, and less dependable than the first-born child in the family. Frequently, the first-born child spends considerable effort attempting to make the younger brother or sister feel guilty about acting like a normal middle-born child. For that first-born child, "normal behavior" is that of a typical first-born. First-born children often include a large number of "oughts" and "shoulds" in their vocabularies, and these words can be very useful in making other people feel guilty about being normal.

In other words, we are more likely to be able to respond creatively to behavior patterns that disturb us if we can recognize that many of these are normal and predictable.

The second basic assumption in this chapter is that guilt is rarely a creative method for motivating people, yet it is widely used in the churches. One method of reducing the use of guilt in motivating people is to recognize that certain patterns of individual and institutional behavior are normal and predictable, even though these patterns do not coincide with our "oughts" and "shoulds" or what we desire to see happen. Another means of reducing the emphasis on the use of guilt in motivating people is to learn to be more aware of the pattern and thus to alternative means of motivating people. (For an elaboration of this concept see the last section of this chapter.)

Clichés for Inducing Guilt

It may be helpful to review several of the most widely used clichés for creating unnecessary, and often counterproductive, guilt among people before moving on to a discussion of how the creation of feelings of guilt often is structured into how a congregation is organized.

1. Perhaps the most widespread of these is the ancient cliché that every congregation should focus its ministry on the people living or working in the neighborhood around the church building. Serve Your Community! has produced a tremendous amount of frustration, guilt, and counterproductive programming. Its history can be traced back first to the writings of a pioneering and influential social theorist, Charles Horton Cooley, who identified the family, playmates, and geographical neighborhood to be the basic primary groups for people.[1] The concept of the "neighborhood unit" as a basic building block in creating urban communities was first explicitly stated in 1923 by Clarence Perry, who defined the size in terms of area and population, the nature of the boundaries, and other characteristics of the ideal urban neighborhood.[2]

While they did not define the neighborhood-unit concept as precisely as Perry did, the leaders in what came to be called the Garden City Movement crusaded for the idea of creating relatively small, homogeneous urban communities as the best approach to planned urban growth. Professional planners adopted the concept as an essential element for the physical design of a city. It was reinforced by the studies of the rural sociologists of the 1920s and 1930s who found that in rural communities the interrelatedness of work, kinship ties, social class, religious affiliation, national origin, language, occupation, and leisure time activities often produced a cohesive and unified experience of community. Urban planners, real estate developers, church leaders, educational leaders, and sociologists have attempted to apply the neighborhood unit concept, which flourished in many rural areas, to the development of the far more heterogeneous urban residential communities. The concept was used in the development of a whole series of "new towns" from Riverside, Illinois (1869); Pullman, Illinois (1880); Radburn, New Jersey (1928); the Greenbelt communities of the late 1930s; Reston, Virginia (1963); and Columbia, Maryland (1964). Planners were very reluctant to give up on the idea that people should and would work, socialize, neighbor, attend church, shop, attend school, and participate in leisure time and recreational activities in the same geographical neighborhood where they resided.

By 1950, however, researchers were beginning to discover that the neighborhood-unit concept was a fallacious and misleadingly simple explanation of the dynamics of urban life.[3] While it was still widely used by planners and the designers of new towns, the concept of the homogeneous urban neighborhood began to come under severe attack as an unrealistic, racist, segregationist, anti-egalitarian, and restrictive concept during the 1960s.[4] The findings of the serious researchers pointed out that in urban America people did not socialize with their neighbors, most of them did not see their neighbors at work, and increasingly people left the place of residence to attend church, to worship, and to participate in social and leisure time activities. When people change their place of residence (during the average five-year period 44 percent of the American population, age 5 and over, will change their place of residence at least once, and 56 percent will remain in the same dwelling, but less than one-half of the movers will move across a county line), they tend to continue their affiliation with the congregation with which they have been members rather than transfer their membership to a different congregation. In general, in urban and suburban America people socialize first with their kinfolk, second with people they meet at work or through their profession, third with people they meet in voluntary organizations and through leisure time activities, and fourth with their geographical neighbors. The only major exceptions to that generalization are (a) first generation Americans and (b) the first residents of new housing units.

Thus the advice to a long-established urban congregation meeting in a building in a neighborhood where none of the housing is occupied by the original residents is diversionary nonsense. Perhaps the worst theological component in this cliché is the emphasis on defining community in geographical terms rather than as experience. The Christian congregation should be perceived as a called-out community of believers who experience a

144

shared sense of community, not as a collection of people who happen to reside in the same neighborhood. The response of people to a Christian congregation should be based on the challenge of a common religious commitment, not on the place of residence. Rather than talk about mission and outreach in terms of land and buildings, it usually is more productive to think and plan in terms of the unmet needs of people outside any worshiping congregation.

Rather than make church members feel guilty about not reaching and ministering to all of the people living near the meeting place, it might be better to identify the common characteristics of those congregations which do function as geographical parishes. This is not difficult to do. There are hundreds of these, including the nationality Roman Catholic parishes in Chicago, the French Roman Catholic parishes in Louisiana, some Reformed Church in America and Christian Reformed Church congregations in Michigan and Iowa, several German Lutheran parishes in Wisconsin and Texas, and the Amish congregations in Pennsylvania. These are examples of congregations ministering to all, or nearly all the residents surrounding the meeting place. These congregations also illustrate that for a congregation to "serve the people in the neighborhood" usually means a comparatively homogeneous collection of members serving a geographical community of people who "are pretty much like us."

By contrast, the normal pattern is for a congregation to serve a group of people who can be identified by such common characteristics as denominational heritage, social class, racial or language or nationality background, level of competence in verbal skills, place on the theological spectrum, or personal religious experiences rather than by their place of residence.

The injunction "Serve Your Community!" is a simplistic and guilt-inducing cliché which runs counter to the normal experiences of the typical Christian congregation on the North American continent. Its application tends to produce frustration and guilt rather than an effective evangelistic outreach of meaningful service ministries.

2. Closely related to this is another guilt-inducing cliché. This is the oft-repeated ideal that every Christian congregation should include people from all of the racial, social, economic, educational, ethnic, occupational, and age brackets and compartments of society. The validity of this ideal has been demolished by the proponents of "the homogeneous unit" in the Church Growth Movement,[5] but it continues to be a widely articulated goal of many church leaders. The truly homogeneous congregation tends to be comparatively rare, and when it is encountered, it usually is either (a) declining in membership or (b) a skillfully managed collection of relatively homogeneous subgroups of people. This fact of life often evokes the response, "But it shouldn't be that way."

These two ideals of serving a narrowly defined geographical community of people and of developing a highly heterogeneous membership often are projected as twin goals by the same person. Experience suggests it is rare for any congregation to achieve either one and almost impossible to accomplish both. Thus the acceptance of these clichés as congregational goals is almost certain to produce either one or two loads of guilt for the average congregation.

3. A third, and widely used guilt-inducing cliché was illustrated in the opening paragraph of this chapter. This is to equate the vows made by a person in uniting with a congregation with the gifts, talents, and skills required for teaching Sunday school. In addition to being contrary to the teachings of St. Paul and Martin Luther that different individuals have different God-given talents and vocations, the words suggest that if a listener does not respond affirmatively, that individual probably is not really a committed Christian.

Furthermore, the technique used is one that tends to arouse guilt and hostility rather than to produce volunteers. The effective method for recruiting volunteers is to contact prospective candidates individually and directly on a person-to-person basis, rather than to make a mass appeal.

Finally, what if one or two or three persons in the congregation do volunteer in response to that mass appeal, but none of them is considered to be an acceptable prospective teacher? Will an additional load of guilt and rejection be placed on them when they are told that they do not meet the qualifications required of a teacher?

4. One of the more subtle, but also more widespread and counterproductive methods of inducing guilt is to ask the members of a circle in the women's organization or the members of an adult class to switch to a new group in order to follow a directive from headquarters to rotate the members of adult groups. Typically many of the adults involved, especially the older ones, will be very reluctant to make the change. They are now in a group with two or three or four close friends, they are completely out of practice in the art of making new friends, and they would prefer to remain with their old friends.

Most congregations offer these adults four choices. They can "go along," lose touch with longtime and treasured friends, and feel guilty about not staying in closer contact with their old friends. They can drop out and feel guilty about dropping out. They can lie by offering some excuse, such as the dependence on a friend for a ride, why they cannot move to a different group and subsequently feel guilty about telling a lie. Or they can resist the proposal for playing "fruit basket upset" and feel guilty about not loyally following the commandments from headquarters.

5. While it has been used by only a small fraction of all religious congregations on the continent, one of the most effective methods for inducing guilt is the long range master plan for construction of a new meeting place. A typical example of this was described in the third illustration in the beginning of this chapter.

The process is a relatively simple one. One generation of optimistic and enthusiastic church leaders develops a proposal for a church building to be implemented by subsequent generations. This master plan usually is divided into three or four stages for implementation. Several years later and frequently fifteen or twenty or thirty years later, it turns out that conditions have changed. The growth curve of the congregation did not reach the predicted level forecast for it. The nature of the congregation has changed, and frequently it is more heterogeneous and pluralistic than was anticipated. Building costs have increased at a fantastic rate. As a result of these and other changes, several people now have serious reservations about building that last unit (usually a sanctuary, but sometimes a youth building or a recreation center or a school).

Many of the newer members, and perhaps even the recently arrived pastor, who had no part in preparing the original master plan, can dispose of the issue very easily. "Let's not build it." The longtime members, however, and especially those who were very influential in preparing the master plan or those who have a deep loyalty to the minister who spearheaded that early dream, cannot dismiss it that easily. What happens? In some congregations the master plan is not completed, and the longtime members go to their graves still feeling guilty about not keeping faith with the commitment they had made to God and/or that master plan. In other congregations the final unit is constructed almost exactly as it was planned twenty years earlier. Subsequently the members feel guilty about having spent all that money to construct what has turned out to be an empty building. It is a memorial, not to the glory of God, but to an excessively ambitious master plan.

6. Another method of inducing guilt that is used in the vast majority of congregations is to make people feel guilty about not wanting to sit in the front pews. As was explained in the first chapter, the reason most churchgoers prefer not to sit in the front pews is that they are normal. In a large group gathering the best seats are in the back rows and next to the aisles. The worst seats are in the front row. Normal people prefer the best seats over the worse seats.

7. During the 1950s the family-centered church was held up as the American ideal, and many people still see that as the ideal. At Trinity Church as the members begin to grow older and as their children leave home, the congregation begins to reflect the effects, and gradually a growing proportion of the members are widowed, divorced, or couples without young children at home. The children's department of the Sunday school declines in size. Several of the attractive rooms in the church school wing that was added in 1959 (to accommodate the huge number of young

children in the Sunday school in 1955) are now empty. No longer are there enough interested teen-agers to form a youth choir. Anyone sitting in the balcony, although it is seldom open now, looks down on a large number of white-haired or bald heads. Gradually the longtime members at Trinity begin to feel guilty about not living up to the image of being a family church. Someone goes over the membership roll and discovers that only a fifth of the adult (age 18 and over) members come from homes composed of a husband and wife with children under eighteen at home (see page 113). This causes many members to have even stronger guilt feelings. So when the fifty-three-year-old minister leaves (his youngest child is now 22 and has just graduated from college), Trinity Church seeks a young minister with one wife and two very young children. The people feel less guilty now as they see the young pastor in the chancel every Sunday and see his young wife and the two children talking with parishioners in the corridors. They have done their part, they have employed a young minister with a lovely family. Before long Trinity once again will be a congregation filled with young families!

As the months roll by, the number of young families does increase. It turns out that this young preacher has a unique gift in relating to children and to youth, and they respond. Instead of three or four children and a half dozen teen-agers attending the Sunday morning worship service, on the typical Sunday morning there are fifteen to eighteen youth sitting down front in the center section of pews while off to the side there usually are ten to twelve fifth-, sixth-, seventh-, and eighth-graders sitting together. As this pattern continues and is clearly affirmed by the new young minister, several of the ushers begin to grumble. They were reared in a culture that taught that the children should sit and worship in the same pew with their parents. That is obviously as it should be, why else would a church install those long pews? The ushers begin to feel guilty that somehow their church is dividing families rather than reinforcing family ties. When visitors attend, they see sections of pews filled largely by adults while other sections are occupied by children or youth. How will that help visitors and prospective members recognize that we're a family church? At Trinity, as in many other congregations, some people are able to generate feelings of guilt even about good news.

Structuring in Guilt

One means of inducing counterproductive guilt among the members is by the use of some of the traditional clichés described here. Another means of inducing guilt is to build the mechanism into the organizational structure and decision-making processes of a congregation. This structured-in guilt can be illustrated by a half dozen common examples.

1. A very common approach is the "unlimited tenure system." This causes the members who are asked to serve as workers or leaders in the church to initiate their own termination date. For some people, this is very easy. For others, however, to announce "I will not be able to teach Sunday school next year" or "I must resign from this job" is a very difficult problem. Some continue year after year and feel guilty about not being able to perform more effectively in that position or they continue and feel guilty about neglecting other responsibilities and/or their family. In either case placing the responsibility on the member for terminating a particular responsibility often is a very effective means of inducing guilt. It also is a means of causing some overworked volunteers to drop out of the church completely. They feel so guilty about not being able to meet expectations that they find it easier to drop out completely rather than continuing at a lower level of participation and regularly being reminded of how guilty they feel because they are doing less than they used to do.

2. Closely related to this is the use of guilt as a motivating factor in causing members to accept a job in the church when that person insists he/she does not have the competence and/or time for that particular responsibility.

3. In some congregations, guilt, rather than love of the Lord, is the basic motivating force used to increase the level of giving by members or to encourage the members to contribute to special causes.

4. One of the more subtle forms of creating guilt comes with the

departure of the pastor who is loved and held in high esteem by the members. The members feel a sense of grief when they learn their minister is leaving. "It's almost like losing a member of my family," exclaimed one member when she heard her pastor was leaving.

Three of the guilt-inducing responses to this natural grief are widely used by clergy. One is the statement by the departing minister, "I love you all, but remember, after today I cease to be your pastor. Please forget about me and love and support your new minister as you have supported me these past years." The second is used by the denominational executive who admonishes the members to immediately transfer their love and loyalty from their departing pastor to the new minister. The third of this series is offered by the newly arrived minister who may cause the members to feel guilty because they still express strong favorable feelings toward "good old Reverend Jones." If the new minister cannot do this alone, there usually are several lay leaders who will help members feel guilty because they still feel a sense of loss over the departure of the previous pastor.

5. A more subtle means of inducing guilt is accomplished by articulating goals for the coming year in vague, general, and/or extravagant terms without precisely identifying who had agreed to be responsible for implementing each goal.

This means that when the goal is not achieved because it has been articulated in vague terms or because the responsibility for implementation has not been agreed upon by all concerned, the entire congregation will experience a sense of guilt-producing frustration and failure.

6. One of the most widely-used sentences in the area of intercongregational relationships is "We ought to do more together." This is a means of either (a) causing people to feel guilty about not being more actively involved in intercongregational cooperation and/or (b) using guilt as the basic motivating force for inter-church cooperation. Either result usually is a loser.

How does your church make people feel guilty? Are the results counterproductive? Or have we made you feel guilty by bringing up this subject?

Creating Low Morale

Just as guilt tends to be counterproductive when it is used to motivate people, low morale tends to provide a negative climate for planning. Frequently the first step in any systematic effort in planning for a church's ministry must be to respond to a low level of self-esteem (see pages 101-3). Another approach to that issue, which overlaps the subject of counterproductive guilt, is to identify some of the more frequent causes of low morale in a congregation. If these causes can be identifed, it may be possible to avoid creating or increasing low morale in a congregation. It may even be possible to begin to eliminate the problem by eliminating the causes! Here are several common causes of low morale resulting from certain leadership patterns.

The first on this list, and one of the most widely used means of creating low morale, is to set impossible goals.

"Our goal is to have every member in church on every Sunday morning during Lent," declared Frank Jenkins with tremendous enthusiasm in his voice one February evening. "If the minister will cooperate by preaching challenging and inspiring sermons, we can do it," he added as he discussed this goal with other members of the Board of this 229-confirmed-member congregation.

"That's not realistic," objected Harry Rizzo. "With the children we have nearly 300 baptized members, and our new sanctuary will only seat 225, including the choir loft. Why don't we set our attendance goal as an average of 225 during Lent? That's higher than it has ever been here."

"Nope! I won't settle for less than perfection!" replied Frank Jenkins. "We can put chairs in back and in the aisles, and it won't hurt for the latecomers to have to stand. That'll make them get here earlier the next Sunday."

Frank Jenkins won the rest of the Board to his point of view, and his goal was adopted. The actual attendance during Lent averaged 244 each Sunday morning, despite a siege of bad weather and an above average amount of sickness in the congregation. Frank tried to convince his fellow leaders that "If we had better preaching here, we would have achieved our goal."

GUILT, MORALE, AND MOTIVATION

A second means of creating low morale was developed by the Republicans in the presidential election of 1948 and used by the Democrats twenty years later. It often is referred to as snatching defeat from the jaws of victory. Frank Jenkins used this technique in the congregation which has just been described.

After that congregation had completed construction of the new sanctuary, they remodeled the sixty-three-year-old former sanctuary into a large and very attractive fellowship hall and installed a new kitchen in what had been a classroom on one side of the sanctuary. Visitors, denominational staff members, and several recent new members were very favorably impressed with the results. Frank Jenkins, however, explained to everyone that the kitchen was a "disaster" and very poorly designed. Soon others began to complain about the colors that were used in painting it; a few complained that the new ceiling was too low, but some thought it was too high. Several members did not like the carpet, and a dozen or so complained about the banners that had been made by the youth group to add a little color to the room.

Sometimes these two techniques are combined by setting an exceptionally high goal in a financial campaign and then treating the result as a defeat when the final total is nine-tenths of the goal, but far above what the vast majority had believed to be possible. This is usually a very effective means of creating low morale in a congregation.

While some people enjoy the unexpected, confronting church members with unpleasant surprises is a third method some leaders use to lower morale.

"Come on! Let's get over to the car and get on home," scolded the twenty-six-year-old mother to her three-year-old son as she hurried across the parking lot to her car at 11:30 one Sunday morning. An acquaintance greeted her as he walked to his car in the church parking lot, and she explained, "They just told me I'm supposed to be back here at 12 o'clock to help serve the meal. This is the first I've heard of it. I have a half hour to get home, find a baby-sitter, fix Jimmy's lunch, and get back here! I had agreed to help with the evening meal for this all-day affair, but the woman in charge just told me they had cancelled that, and now I'm supposed to help with the luncheon."

This same technique can be seen when the "successful" campaign to retire the last of the indebtedness has been completed—and then the members are told there still remains an $18,000 loan to the denomination. This had been overlooked in the effort to pay off the bank loan so the congregation really is not completely debt free. The same procedure for undercutting congregational morale was used in many church-related housing-for-the-elderly programs in which the congregation was assured that if they could raise several thousand dollars in "seed money" that would be the end of their obligation. Later they found themselves committed to raising an additional $30,000 or $60,000 or $100,000 to complete the project.

Other forms of unpleasant surprises include advancing the time of the event at the last minute or cancelling a traditional event on which many members had invested hours of time and an unmeasured amount of energy or the sudden and completely unexpected resignation of the pastor halfway through the building program that he had initiated.

This same leadership style often is very proficient at using guilt and a variety of other forms of blackmail to influence the decision-making process. This may include the repeated use of "If you're really a Christian, you will do this," or "Only a racist would oppose that," or "If you really love this church, you will support this" or "If you have any concern for the youth of this church, you will attend this event," or "This program will sort out the Sunday Christians from those who really love the Lord."

The use of these and related forms of blackmail obviously are incompatible with the teachings of Jesus, but they are very effective means of undercutting morale.

Occasionally this same basic leadership style is expressed in another form which is illustrated by this brief conversation.

"I have the feeling that I've been had!" exclaimed Dick Burns as he walked out of a church meeting with his friend, Jim Hallahan. "Me, too," replied Jim. "And this is the last time anyone will get me to this kind of event."

154

One of the most effective methods for undercutting morale is for the people attending a church meeting to leave feeling they have been manipulated. Sometimes this is done by the use of guilt or blackmail to secure support for a weak proposal. Not infrequently it is the "spiritualize the problem" technique in which the leaders ask everyone to pause and pray for God's guidance and the prayer is for God to lead the recalcitrants into agreeing with and supporting the decision which the leaders have already committed themselves to, but now find themselves lacking the necessary support from the members.

Perhaps the most devastating impact on morale in the church comes when people suddenly discover they no longer can trust one or more leaders.

This may happen when the treasurer embezzles church funds or when the minister exercises very poor judgment on a major issue or when the Board violates the trust placed in it by the members or when the leaders set goals which are completely incompatible with the expectations of the members or when it is discovered that a disaster could have been prevented if the leaders had been more open and forthright in their public statements about a particular problem or when the leaders lie in order to "cover up" a situation which cannot be covered up.

This usually means the successors have to concentrate their efforts on restoring the trust of the people in that particular office before they are free to carry out the duties of the office.

Sometimes the best approach to problems of low morale is to avoid the methods and techniques which tend to create low morale.

How Do You Motivate?

If guilt is a counterproductive method for motivating people and if certain leadership styles and actions undermine the morale of a congregation, what are some healthier alternatives? There are many different responses to that question, and several of these can be illustrated very quickly.

The cardboard replica of a giant thermometer in the narthex at

Trinity Church reported the progress in securing pledges to the building fund campaign. Every week the red vertical column in the center of this reporting device climbed higher and higher. Finally it climbed past the 100 percent mark. The building fund drive had been concluded successfully!

"We are asking if you would be willing to serve on a special committee to plan and to be responsible for our annual all-church picnic on June 17," Jerry Rogers asked a young couple who had united with Grace Church a few months earlier. "I understand that you just moved here from Wyoming, and this also will be an opportunity for you to make some new friends here in this congregation. Paul and Lois Brice, who served on the picnic committee last year, have agreed to chair this year's committee so you'll have the guidance of some folks who know what's involved. Your responsibilities will end on the evening of June 17. Would you be interested in helping?"

"Before we ask Paul to dismiss us with the benediction, I would like to take a minute or two and review what we accomplished here tonight," declared Chuck Harper, president of the church council at Bethany Church. He then proceeded to list each of the decisions that had been made, to review the agreement that had been achieved on five other items, to summarize the progress that had been achieved during the discussion of two proposals that had been postponed for a decision until next month, and to commend each of the six committee representatives for their reports. He concluded this summary by lifting up what had been for him the most significant learning experience of the evening. As they drove home together after that night's meeting, Bill Cole said to his neighbor, Dick Palmer, "I certainly am glad we elected Chuck as president of the church council. This is my third hitch on the council, and I can't remember when we got so much done in one evening as we do under Chuck's leadership." "You're right," agreed Dick Palmer. "Chuck has a great sense of humor, he always summarizes what we have accomplished before we leave, and he places great emphasis on making sure that each council meeting is a learning experience for everyone present."

"We're convinced you would be a tremendous teacher in our

children's department in the Sunday school," declared a member
of the Christian education committee to Sally Vogel one spring
day. "Before you decide, however, either to accept or refuse our
request to teach next fall, we would like to ask you to do three
things. First, we would like to have you spend four Sundays with
Ruth Hartwell and Joyce Vitale, who are now team teaching the
third- and fourth-grade class. That will give you a feel for the
situation. Second, there will be a lab school experience for
prospective new teachers at Central Church in early June, and we
hope you will be able to participate in that experience. Third, we
want you to become a part of our Christian education committee.
That committee not only acts as a program committee in planning
the educational ministry here in our church, it also serves as a
support group for all the teachers."

What do these four incidents have in common? Together they
illustrate six creative approaches in the motivation of lay
volunteers.

Feedback

Why do people enjoy playing golf or bowling? One reason is that
they receive an immediate report back on their performance. Or,
reflect on this brief conversation. "How did the meeting go last
night?" "Great, we had the biggest crowd of the year!" A quick and
easy means of evaluating a meeting is to measure the size of the
attendance. People want rapid feedback on the evaluation of
performance. This was the basic reason for placing those wooden
plaques on the walls of thousands of churches which reported (1)
attendance a year ago, (2) attendance last week, (3) attendance
today, (4) offering a year ago, (5) offering last week, (6) offering
today. One method of motivating people is to provide an
immediate feedback evaluating performance. This may be in the
form of a cardboard thermometer reporting progress on a building
fund campaign or a pat on the back or a kind word or applause or an
oral progress report or by serving as an "insider" where one knows
what is happening as a result of this direct involvement. How do

157

EFFECTIVE CHURCH PLANNING

you provide for the immediate feedback to members on what is happening in your congregation?

Terminal Date

In some congregations an affirmative response to a request to teach Sunday school or to serve as a volunteer leader may mean a "lifetime sentence." In an increasing number of churches, however, the value of setting a precise date when the volunteer's responsibility will end is being recognized. This task force approach with a clearly defined reponsibility and a precise terminal date is especially useful in encouraging new members to become involved in the life of a congregation where they may not know many people and thus feel like uncomfortable "outsiders" who find it easier to say no than to accept responsibilities in a strange and uncertain setting. The use of precisely defined terminal dates also is helpful in securing commitments from tightly scheduled and very busy people.

Satisfactions

Experience strongly suggests that attendance at meetings will be higher if people can look forward to that meeting, knowing from past experiences that they will (a) leave feeling that something has been accomplished as a result of their investment of time and energy, (b) enjoy themselves (humor is the best lubricant for getting through a long or difficult meeting), and (c) learn something useful and/or interesting during the course of the meeting. These satisfactions encourage people to return for the next meeting. Do people gain these satisfactions from the meetings in your church?

Support

The chances of securing an affirmative response from a prospective volunteer teacher, worker, or leader in the church will be greatly enhanced if the person asked (a) feels self-confident about accepting that responsibility, (b) feels competent to carry out the assignment, and (c) is assured of the reinforcement of some type of support groups and knows he or she will not be left in complete isolation. (This also is a means of increasing the sense of satisfaction the volunteer gains from a responsibility.)

One method of accomplishing this is to ask two people to co-chair a committee or to encourage two or three or four individuals to teach as a team or to urge six to twelve adults to function as a team of counselors for a junior high youth group. Another approach was illustrated earlier when Sally Vogel was asked to be a teacher in the children's department. It was assumed that her competence would be strengthened by observing two experienced teachers and by attending a lab school. As her sense of competence rose, her self-confidence would be increased. Finally, in that church every teacher is a member of the Christian education committee since there is no other mutual support group for teachers.

Theories X and Y

In one of the most influential essays ever written, Douglas MacGregor described two different theories of motivation. The centuries-old approach has been to motivate people by a system of rewards and punishments or the carrot-and-stick approach. This he called Theory X. MacGregor proposed that a better approach would be what he described as Theory Y—to motivate people by encouraging commitment through participation, the satisfaction of self-actualizing needs, and the acceptance of responsibility. (This essay was expanded into the famous book *The Human Side of Enterprise*, 1960.)

Since most congregations are organized with a governing board designed to tell the members what they can and cannot do, it may appear to be difficult to apply Theory Y. This difficulty is increased by the fact that many congregations have trained the members to expect other people to tell them what they should do or not do. It is assumed that the governing board is to accept responsibility, and the whole system of the governance of the congregation is based on trusting an elite group of old-timers or active members and

159

distrusting the rest of the members. Unless and until the congregation is reorganized on a different set of assumptions, it will be difficult to apply MacGregor's Theory Y although a significant step in that direction was taken when Jerry Rogers asked a young couple at Grace Church to help plan and be responsible for the all-church picnic.

Which Button?

Today it is possible to see in many congregations the consequences of three different approaches used during the 1960s to motivate congregations to become more actively involved in community ministries, social action, neighborhood outreach, civil rights, and the attack on poverty. In retrospect the events of the 1960s offer a context for suggesting alternatives to the use of guilt as a motivating technique.

In some congregations the method was to attempt to motivate by making people feel guilty about who they were and what they were and were not doing. In others the emphasis appears to have been in a legalistic approach to what is required of a Christian. In a third group of congregations the approach was to attempt to emphasize the two great commandments of Jesus to love the Lord and love one's neighbor.

What happened?

Eight or ten years later it appears that the fruits of motivating by pushing the "guilt" button have turned out to be deep and lasting hostility. The efforts to use a legalistic approach to motivation appear to have produced divisive and destructive conflict. By contrast, the efforts to motivate people through an emphasis on neighbor-centered love have produced healthy fruits.

Which button do you push when you seek to motivate people? What is the impact on the guilt level of the people? On the morale of the congregation? What is the feedback system? Do you use terminal dates? What are the consequences in creating new opportunities for the personal and spiritual growth of the members? Does your technique raise the level of satisfactions of the volunteers?

7

The Enabler:
An Impossible Challenge?

"Listen to how this minister describes his leadership style," suggested one of the members of the pulpit nominating committee at St. Andrew's Church. The nine members of this committee were together for their fifth meeting since they had been chosen to recommend a new pastor for this 646-member congregation. They had the dossiers of several promising candidates, and at this meeting they were seeking to narrow down the list of possibilities. "He writes that he sees himself as an enabler, he is willing to allow people to fail, and he believes that the basic leadership responsibilities in a congregation should rest on the laity. He sees the role of the pastor as being one who equips the saints to carry out the ministry of the church."

"That sounds interesting," responded the youngest member of the committee. "I think maybe that's the leadership style we should be looking for here. I've always felt both of our last two pastors were a little too dictatorial, especially Dr. Anderson. Maybe we should be looking for a minister who doesn't try to run everything by himself, but believes in and trusts the laity. I think he deserves serious consideration."

"How large is the congregation he's serving now?" inquired Randy Hamilton, who was a professor of social work at the nearby university.

"According to this sheet, he is in his second full-time pastorate and in his fifth year as the pastor of a congregation of 261 members," came the reply.

"I doubt if he's the person we're looking for," responded Dr. Hamilton. "It's one thing to try to be an enabler in a congregation of two or three hundred members, but something quite different to serve as the pastor in a church as large as this one. We need a leader, an initiator, a take-charge type personality here at St. Andrew's."

"I'm inclined to agree with you, Randy," added Joe Frederickson. "We just moved here three years ago, and about seven or eight years earlier I served on the pulpit committee in the church we were in back there. We called a self-identified enabler type minister, and we got burned. We found that the word enabler was a synonym for not being an initiator, not calling, not being aggressive, and not taking leadership responsibilities. Whenever a complaint came up about what the minister wasn't doing, his response always was 'But I am not supposed to do that. That should be done by the laity. My job is to enable the laity to be ministers rather than to do everything myself.' Preaching, funerals, baptisms, and weddings were about the only things he ever agreed were his responsibilities."

"But I thought the seminaries were all encouraging the students to see themselves as enablers," questioned Nancy Rosario. "Isn't that the leadership style now being taught in the theological seminaries to people going into the ministry?"

"Not anymore," replied Randy Hamilton. "That was the 1960s emphasis. Today the emphasis is that leaders do lead, they initiate, and they organize. They're taught that while a leader is not expected do everything, leaders do cause things to happen. They're taught to take a more active role than was a part of the old enabler theory of leadership style."[1]

This conversation illustrates one of the most neglected points of tension in the church: What is the appropriate leadership style for a pastor?

For many years the concept of the pastor as an enabler, as the one responsible for equipping the saints for ministry (Eph. 4:12), as a person who facilitated the blossoming of the laity, and as an individual who nurtured the gifts of the laity, was one of the most popular concepts in describing ministerial leadership styles. For some it appears to be the ideal leadership role for a pastor. While it is impossible to affix precise dates on trends such as this one, it appears that the concept of the pastor as an enabler peaked in popularity in the late 1960s and has been declining ever since. The concept still has wide support, however, and is still being advocated by many as the ideal role for a pastor by many professional (and professorial) preacher-watchers.

At this point is may be of value to reflect on three questions about the rise and decline of the enabler as the ideal leadership role for a pastor.

Why the Decline?

There are several reasons for the apparent declining interest in the concept of the minister as the enabler. The first of these, which will be discussed in more detail subsequently, is that it is the most demanding and difficult leadership role for a pastor to fill.

The second reason for the apparent decline is that, as happens so often, the concept was oversold as a universal response that would apply to all pastors and to all congregations. A more realistic analysis reveals that at different points in their history, congregations need different leadership gifts, talents, and skills in their pastor. What may be appropriate at one point may not be the appropriate combination at a later stage of that congregation's history. Likewise ministers come not only in different sizes, they also come with different combinations of personalities, skills, experiences, and interests. The enabler role is simply one of a large number of alternative leadership styles open to pastors, and it would be an amazing coincidence if it were the style or role that was compatible with the competence and preference of more than a fraction of all ministers. The Big Revolution of the post–World War II era has been the shift from training people to fit into existing patterns, traditions, roles, structures, systems, and institutions to changing the institutions, structures, expectations, roles, and traditions of society to accommodate the differences among people.[2] Therefore it is unreasonable to expect that any one leadership style would appeal to more than a small proportion of ministers or congregations.

A third factor behind the decline in interest in the enabler concept was illustrated in the conversation at the beginning of this chapter. It is possible for a pastor to specialize as an enabler in a congregation with fewer than a couple hundred members, but most larger conregations demand a stronger and more directive leadership role from the pastor. In general, the larger the congregation, the less time the pastor has for an enabler role, the more difficult it is to carry out that role because of the varying needs of the people, and the greater the pressure from the members for a more aggressive and directive leadership.

Perhaps the most subtle factor behind the declining interest in the enabler role resulted from a neglect of organizational theory. Frequently the newly arrived pastor who sought to function as an enabler was trying to fill a vacancy that did not exist. The previous organizational history of that congregation had created a substantially different set of expectations of the person filling the role of pastor. Unless that organizational context was changed and replaced by a new set of expectations by the members of the pastor's role and responsibilities, the new pastor who sought to function as an enabler was almost certain to become very frustrated. For many would-be enablers this has meant that the first three or four years must be spent as an expert in organization development before the situation was ready for the enabler. Some ministers did not possess these skills. Others did not have the patience. Many did not stay that long. Thus the frustration produced by the minister who sought to be an enabler in a congregational context which demanded a different leadership role of the minister has become a major factor in the declining interest in the concept.

A fifth, and rapidly growing reason for the declining interest in the enabler style of ministerial leadership has been the Church Growth Movement, which became the fastest growing phenomenon on the church scene during the 1970s. Most of the research coming out of the Church Growth Movement emphasized the central importance of a dynamic, aggressive, directive, and evangelistic leadership style by the pastor if a congregation is to grow in size. This contrasts very sharply with the usual definitions of the enabler style.

Closely related to this, and one of the most influential reasons for the declining interest in the enabler concept, has been the negative response of the laity. Congregational leaders usually place a much higher value on the numerical growth of a congregation than they assign to the personal and spiritual growth of the members or to the satisfactions a pastor derives from his or her leadership style. In simple terms, the typical congregational reward system places a high premium on the ministerial leadership qualities which produce a rapid increase in the size of the congregation, and a much lower premium on the ministerial skills which cause individuals to blossom in unexpected but beautiful ways.

When lay leaders are given a choice among five or six different ministerial leadership roles, the enabler style rarely ranks higher than third or fourth or fifth. Most lay leaders prefer a much more aggressive and directive leadership role in their pastor.

A seventh factor behind the declining interest in the enabler can be found in the calendar. The most effective enablers usually find it necessary to retrain the congregation for that style of ministerial leadership. This may require two to five years. Subsequently, the process of "equipping the saints" may take another two or three years before the results become highly visible. Very few lay people, however, are willing to wait four or five years before beginning an evaluation of the pastor's leadership. One result is that some enablers move on before completing their task. Another is that for many of the laity the word "enabler" has become a synonym for "lazy" or "ineffective" or "irresponsible." By contrast, the results from a more authoritarian or aggressive leadership style tend to be more visible far sooner after the arrival of a new pastor. Part of the problem is that some pastors have redefined the word enabler simply to mean "non-directive."

Finally, the churches do reflect much of what is happening in the total society, and the 1970s brought a demand for a more aggressive, dynamic, anticipatory, creative, innovative, and active leadership style than that offered by the typical enabler.

EFFECTIVE CHURCH PLANNING
Why So Difficult?

Far more significant than the declining interest in the churches in the enabler role for a pastor is the question, Why is this such a difficult ministerial leadership role and style?

The basic response to that question is very simple. It is the most demanding of all alternatives and requires a higher level of competence and more gifts, talents, and skills than any other leadership model!

The non-directive approach to pastoral counseling is a relatively undemanding model and comparatively easy to teach and to learn. It is designed to minimize the amount of harm an unskilled minister may do in difficult counseling situations. By contrast, the enabler model of ministerial leadership is extremely demanding. The minister who chooses this leadership model must be an unusually secure person who has a strong professional identity and is emotionally able to let others receive credit for what has been accomplished. The effective enabler style pastor is able both to stand outside the church system and evaluate what is happening and also be a part of that system sharing in responsibility, authority, and control over what takes place. The effective enablers also have the endurance and willingness to work long hours week after week. This is especially important during the first few years of a pastorate when it is necessary for the new pastor to offer good preaching, be an effective teacher, serve as a catalyst to cause things to happen, provide good pastoral care for the members, learn the unique characteristics of that congregation, be an effective mediator in the resolution of conflict, serve as an administrator, and be an in-house consultant on organization development. The enabler also must be a good organizer, and especially a skillful *reorganizer*, since the usual organizational structure for congregational self-government is not compatible with the enabler leadership role.[3] This may require maintenance of a truce with the denominational leadership while the system of church government is democratized. The enabler role also requires an extroverted personality and a high level of trust in the potentialities of the laity. The introverted personality or the scholar or the minister who prefers to be in the office rather than out with people probably will not be an effective enabler. The effective enabler sees potentialities in people that they do not see in themselves; this requires spending large amounts of time with the members and being a good listener. This is one reason why it is rare to encounter an effective enabler in a congregation with more than two hundred members. There simply are too many people for the pastor to know each one individually well enough to help each person realize his or her potential. Perhaps the most important single characteristic of the effective enabler is a high level of competence in leadership development with an emphasis on the personal fulfillment of the individual rather than on filling vacancies in the table of organization. This also involves the retraining of the laity to be comfortable with a nontraditional style of ministerial leadership.

That long paragraph can be summarized in one sentence. To be an effective enabler requires a very high level of competence in all areas of the ministry, plus hard work plus a very secure and healthy personality, plus long hours plus patience. That is the basic reason that it is so difficult!

A second major reason that this is such a difficult leadership role to fill is that it is incompatible with the organizational structure that has been developed for most congregations.

The organizational structure found in most Christian congregations on the North American continent has been created to (a) identify one individual as the person in charge, (b) provide a group of people (or sometimes only one individual) who have been set apart to tell the rest of the members what they cannot do, (c) discourage initiative, creativity, and innovation, (d) maintain the status quo, (e) identify the lay offices that have supervision over money and real estate as the most influential lay positions, (f) (frequently) obscure the real decision-making point by either having a large board and/or having two competing points of authority (such as elders and deacons or elders and trustees or council and finance committee or council on ministries and administrative board or consistory and trustees), (g) place a higher priority on institutional survival goals than on ministry goals, (h) encourage long tenure in office and/or reward seniority and tenure,

(i) separate the power to initiate and approve from the power to implement, and (j) emphasize counting the no votes rather than the yes votes.[4] While not every one of these generalizations applies to every congregation, most of them apply to a majority of congregations. This means the newly arrived pastor who expects to function as an enabler must either (a) carry out that leadership role in a hostile institutional environment or (b) change the organizational structure of the congregation. Neither is easy and that is a major reason why the enabling role is such a difficult style of pastoral leadership.

A third reason why this is such a difficult leadership role is that many of the larger congregations are understaffed. It is much easier for a minister to function as an enabler in a two-hundred-member congregation than in a six-hundred-member parish. If the pastor is the only professional program staff member in the six-hundred-member congregation, it is certain that some things will not get done. What will not get done? Typically those things which facilitate the enabler role, such as face-to-face visitation with the members, listening, selecting volunteers for leadership positions on the basis of their potential for growth and enrichment rather than to meet the needs of the institution, the careful assimilation of new members, leadership development, broadening the base of participation, and sharing authority and responsibility in decision-making do not get done, and this inhibits the emergence of the pastor as an enabler.

The most effective enablers seem to appear in disproportionately large numbers as the number-three or number-four (in terms of the pecking order and financial compensation) persons on the staffs of large congregations which, coincidentally, often are perceived by many as "overstaffed."

The combination of tradition and tenure provide another barrier for the would-be enabler. The traditional management structure in most congregations resembles a pyramid with the pastor at or near the top of the pyramid. The enabler style of ministerial leadership requires what often is described as a flat leadership model or as a circle with no head chair at the table. To change from one tradition to a new pattern, to institutionalize the new pattern, to retrain the longtime lay leaders to a new style, and to prove the value of the new pattern by its results, typically requires pastorates of ten to twenty years. In several denominations this almost completely eliminates the possibility of effective enablers, except in very small and newly organized congregations, because of a denominational tradition of short pastorates.

Finally, while it is a generalization that does not apply to all adults, the enabler leadership style is most compatible with the typical personality characteristics of the adult who was reared as a middle-born child in a family of three or more siblings. Since well over one-half of all ordained ministers were reared either (a) as an only child or (b) as first-borns, this suggests the enabler role is not naturally compatible with the majority of the individuals who are called to the professional ministry.

What Is the Future?

If the enabler leadership role and style has been declining in appeal, especially to the laity, and if it is such a difficult role to fill, what does the future hold for this concept?

Perhaps the first positive statement is that the declining popularity of the enabler concept will reduce the creation of unnecessary and counterproductive guilt. When support for the enabler role of ministerial leadership was at its peak, this produced a lot of guilt feelings in the pastor who did not identify himself or herself as an enabler. (Now the social pressure is to make the pastor feel guilty unless the congregation served by that minister is showing a net growth in membership of at least five percent per year.)

Today there also appears to be a shift away from the earlier focus on ministerial leadership styles being evaluated in isolation from specific congregations and a move toward looking at the "match" between the leadership style, the special gifts and talents of the minister, and the needs of that congregation at this point in its history. Among the ramifications of this shift in focus are (a) an affirmation of the distinctive gifts of different ministers, (b) a

169

recognition of the differences among congregations and of their distinctive needs when they seek a new pastor, (c) a greater emphasis on seeking to match resources with needs in ministerial placement, and (d) an affirmation of the legitimacy of a variety of ministerial leadership roles and styles.

A third emerging trend is to shift the focus in evaluating leadership styles. In the 1960s and early 1970s the emphasis was unduly on the comparison between the pastor and the "perfect ministry." A natural and predictable result of this approach was to identify the weaknesses, shortcomings, and liabilities of the pastor being evaluated. Since the enabler model demands a higher level of competence in more areas of personality and performance than any other ministerial leadership model, it exposed many weaknesses in the average pastor. Today the emphasis is gradually shifting toward identifying, affirming, and building on the strengths, gifts, talents, and abilities of the pastor. For example, instead of identifying the weaknesses and shortcomings of a pastor and urging that any continuing education courses be directed at "curing" those weaknesses, there is a growing trend to encourage pastors to spend their continuing education time enhancing their strengths. Among other things, that usually turns out to be more fun and also more productive. Specializing in one's weaknesses tends to feed depression, unhappiness, guilt, frustration, despair, and pessimism.

Finally, as pastors move away from the old pattern of trying to live up to some idealized model of ministry, such as the enabler, and begin to identify, affirm, and build on their own strengths, they tend to develop a leadership style that not only is compatible with a potentialities-based planning model (see pages 95-105), but they also begin to develop an aptitude for identifying, affirming, and building on the strengths and potentialities of individual members of the congregation. Some people call that being an enabler.

Notes

CHAPTER 1

1. For a remarkably comprehensive introduction to the research on small groups that was conducted from 1898 through 1974 see A. Paul Hare, *Handbook of Small Group Research*, 2d ed. (New York: Free Press, 1976). This volume includes a 321 page bibliography on small group research studies.

2. For an interesting discussion of this point see William A. Johnson, "Process Management's Bad Theology." *The Christian Century*, July 7-14, 1976, and the letters to the editors in subsequent issues.

3. For an introduction to the research on the size of groups see Margaret E. Hartford, *Groups in Social Work* (New York: Columbia University Press, 1971), pp. 159-81; Hare, *Handbook*, pp. 214-31; Sidney Verba, *Small Groups and Political Behavior: A Study of Leadership* (Princeton University Press, 1961), pp. 17-60; Martin King Whyte, *Small Groups and Political Rituals in China* (Berkeley: University of California Press, 1974), pp. 15-17; Charles H. Cooley, *Social Organization* (New York: Charles Scribner's Sons, 1909); Clovis Shepherd, *Small Groups* (San Francisco: Chandler Publishing Co., 1964), pp. 3-4; Edwin J. Thomas and Clinton F. Fink, "Effects of Group Size" in A. Paul Hare, et al., *Small Groups: Studies in Social Interaction* (New York: A. A. Knopf, 1965), pp. 525-29.

4. One dividing line in group dynamics is when the size of the group goes above seven persons. Another is when it reaches forty. For a discussion of "The Rule of Forty" see Lyle E. Schaller, *The Decision-Makers* (Nashville: Abingdon, 1974), pp. 61-62.

5. For a more extended discussion of this point, see Lyle E. Schaller, *Assimilating New Members* (Nashville: Abingdon, 1978), pp. 21-36.

6. For an explanation of this distinctive concept see Carl Dudley, *Making the Small Church Effective* (Nashville: Abingdon, 1978).

7. *The Wall Street Journal*, May 26, 1978, p. 32.

8. For an excellent brief discussion of this point see Hartford, *Groups in Social Work*, pp. 155-56.

9. Herbert A. Thelen, *Dynamics of Groups at Work* (Chicago: University of Chicago Press, 1954).

10. Roger G. Barker and Paul V. Gump, *Big School, Small School* (Stanford University Press, 1964), p. 202.

11. Harvey Passow, *Secondary Education Reform: Retrospect and Prospect* (New York: Teachers College Press, 1976).

12. For an elaboration of this use of a task as an assimilating process see Schaller, *Assimilating New Members*, pp. 75-80.

CHAPTER 2

1. This is an expansion of the H. Paul Douglass lecture delivered to the Religious Research Association in Washington, D.C. on October 25, 1974.

2. Susana Duncan, "Mental Maps of New York," *New York*, December 19, 1977, pp. 51-62; Kevin Lynch, *The Image of the City* (Cambridge, Mass.: The Technology Press and Harvard University Press, 1960).

3. *The New York Times*, November 6, 1977.

4. Oscar Newman, *Defensible Space* (New York: The Macmillan Co., 1972).

5. For an explanation of why this is normal behavior, see R. A. Hart and G. T. Moore, "The Development of Spatial Cognition: A Review," in *Image and Environment*, R. M. Downs and D. Stea, eds. (Chicago: Aldine-Atherton, 1973).

6. In responding to the criticisms about the rebuilding of Wilkes-Barre, one resident wrote the *New York Times* Op-Ed editor: "In so doing, he (the critic) has missed the real meaning of this whole situation. We have a population tied to the land by emotions that may be incomprehensible to mobile America."

7. Samuel Floyd Pannabecker, *Ventures of Faith* (Elkhart, Ind.: Mennonite Biblical Seminary, 1975), pp. 60-72.

8. Robert M. Griffin, Jr., "Ethological Concepts for Planning," *Journal of the American Institute of Planners*, January 1969, pp. 54-60. Barrie B. Greenbie, "What Can We Learn from Other Animals?" *Journal of the American Institute of Planners*, May 1971, pp. 162-68. For another review of the implications of ethology for planning, see Richard W. Smith, "Territoriality and Space Planning: Some Limitations and Prospects," *Urban and Social Change Review*, Spring, 1973, pp. 50-58.

9. Edward T. Hall, *The Hidden Dimension* (Garden City, N.Y.: Doubleday & Co., 1966). For an early critical review of Hall's book by a professional planner, see the review by Harry S. Coblenz in *Psychology Today*, March, 1970, pp. 12, 16.

10. Edward T. Hall, *The Silent Language* (Garden City, N.Y.: Doubleday & Co., 1959).

11. Robert Ardrey, *The Territorial Imperative* (New York: Atheneum, 1966).

12. Lionel Tiger and Robin Fox, *The Imperial Animal* (New York: Holt, Rinehart and Winston, 1971).

13. For an excellent and brief introduction to Barker's theory see Robert B. Bechtel, *Enclosing Behavior* (Stroudsburg, Pa.: Dowden, Hutchinson & Ross, 1977), pp. 9-10. See also Roger G. Barker, *Ecological Psychology* (Stanford University Press, 1968); Barker and Gump, *Big School, Small School*; and Roger G. Barker and Herbert F. Wright, *Midwest and Its Children* (Evanston: Row, Peterson, 1955).

14. For a critical study of Barker's basic thesis on a much larger sample see Leonard L. Baird, "Big School, Small School: A Critical Examination of the Hypothesis," *Journal of Educational Psychology*, Vol. 60, pp. 253-60. Baird concluded that participation by high school students in art, music, speech, drama, writing, science, and leadership is more frequent in smaller schools than in larger institutions.

15. Gerald D. Suttles, *The Social Order of the Slum* (The University of Chicago Press, 1968); and *The Social Construction of Communities* (The University of Chicago Press, 1972).

16. Suttles also devotes considerable attention to U. C. Wynne-Edwards, *Animal Dispersion in Relation to Social Behavior* (New York: Hofner, 1962) and William Etkin, *Social Behavior from Fish to Man* (University of Chicago Press, 1967). The serious student of ethology also should see N. Tinbergen, *Social Behavior in Animals: With Specific Reference to Vertebrates* (New York: John Wiley & Sons, 1953), or other writings produced by this pioneer in ethology.

17. Marc Fried, "Grieving for a Lost Home," in *The Urban Condition*, Leonard J. Duhl, ed. (New York: Basic Books, 1963), pp. 151-71.

18. C. M. Deasy, *Design for Human Affairs* (New York: John Wiley & Sons, 1974).

19. Anne-Marie Pollowy, *The Urban Nest* (Stroudsburg, Pa.: Dowden, Hutchinson & Ross, 1977).

20. Gwen Bell, Edwina Randall, and Judith E. R. Roeder, *Urban Environments and Human Behavior* (Stroudsburg, Pa.: Dowden, Hutchinson & Ross, 1976).

21. Deasy, *Human Affairs*, p. 45.

22. John Cassel, "Health Consequences of Population Density and Crowding," in *Rapid Population Growth* (Baltimore: National Academy of Sciences, 1971).

23. Summarized from Barrie B. Greenbie, "Social Territory, Community Health and Urban Planning," *Journal of the American Institute of Planners* (March, 1974), pp. 77-78.

24. Newman, *Defensible Space*.

25. Robert Sommer, *Personal Space* (Englewood Cliffs, N.J.: Prentice-Hall, 1969) and *Tight Spaces: Hard Architecture and How to Humanize It* (Englewood Cliffs, N.J.: Prentice-Hall, 1974).

26. A more technical approach to the problems created by "hard" architecture is Jon Lang et al., *Designing for Human Behavior* (Stroudsburg, Pa.: Dowden, Hutchinson and Ross, 1974).

27. Lyn H. Lofland, *A World of Strangers* (New York: Basic Books, 1973).

28. George Maclay and Humphry Knipe, *The Dominant Man* (New York: Dell Books, 1974).

29. A series of these objections is gathered together in M. F. Ashley Montague, ed., *Man and Aggression* (New York: Oxford University Press, 1968).

30. James C. Coleman, *Youth: Transition to Adulthood* (University of Chicago, 1972).

31. For a description of this type of congregation, see Lyle E. Schaller, *Hey, That's Our Church!* (Nashville: Abingdon, 1975), pp. 51-68.

32. Sommer, *Tight Spaces*, pp. 138-39.

33. Paul Tournier, *A Place for You* (New York: Harper & Row, 1968).

34. One of the other areas of confusion which has had a tremendous and unfortunate impact on church planning also came out of the 1920s. This was the assimilation of rural sociology, and its geographical emphasis on a definition of community, into the studies of urban communities. The result has been that in community sociology in general and in urban church planning in particular, the word "community" has been defined with a major emphasis on territory rather than on the experience of community. For an excellent summary of the classical meanings of community as a social network, rather than as a place, see Thomas Bender, *Community and Social Change in America* (New Brunswick, N.J.: Rutgers University Press, 1978).

35. Barker, *Ecological Psychology*, pp. 19-34.

36. These eight observations are based on the research of A. Wicker, "Size of Church Membership and Members' Support of Church Behavior Settings," *Journal of Personality and Social Psychology*, vol. 13, pp. 278-88; and Barker, *Ecological Psychology*, pp. 200-201.

37. A simple illustration of how the dependency on the pastor can be avoided in large congregations can be found in the thousands of large congregations which have a strong emphasis on the role of the adult Sunday school classes. In many of these large congregations the members find opportunities for need-satisfying behavior which originates within a class and the individual's efforts are rewarded by that class. This minimizes the dependence on the pastor for originating need-satisfying tasks or for rewarding an individual's efforts and thus reduces the pressures for paternalistic leadership by the pastor. The institutional commitment of the individual is to the class or group rather than to the pastor. In these churches which are really congregations of many large groups, short pastorates are rarely disruptive.

NOTES

CHAPTER 3

1. For two alternative responses to the issue of congregational self-esteem see Schaller, *Hey, That's Our Church!* pp. 183-92.

2. Whether there really are finite limitations on these and other resources is a fascinating philosophical question, but most persons born before 1940 and after 1950 have been taught to believe these are finite resources and therefore find it easy, and comfortable, to shift over to an allocative planning model.

3. Almost all the energy to heat a home now comes from the sun. Without the sun, homes would be at minus 273 degrees Celsius, but even in January in Wisconsin the sun will heat the average home to minus 30 degrees Celsius. It is the supplemental heat to bring the temperature up another fifty degrees that is necessary for comfort, but the sun is the primary source for heating that home the first 240 degrees to 300 degrees above the absolute zero (-273° Celsius).

CHAPTER 4

1. While many church leaders are inclined to diagnose a poor level of financial support by the members or "a lack of commitment" as problems, in the overwhelming majority of cases they are symptoms of more basic issues such as poor internal communication or a low level of trust or poor stewardship education or the lack of a channel through which the members can express their commitment. For further reading on this point, see Schaller, *Parish Planning* (Nashville: Abingdon, 1971), pp. 36-64 and 134-41; and *Hey, That's Our Church!* pp. 34-38.

2. For an elaboration of this point see, ibid., 101-10.

CHAPTER 5

1. For an excellent analysis of this, see Dudley, *Making the Small Church Effective*, pp. 32-45.

2. For an elaboration of this concept, see Schaller, *Survival Tactics in the Parish* (Nashville: Abingdon, 1977), pp. 80-90.

3. The descriptive references here apply to the 95 percent of the adult population who are biologically right-handed.

4. For an introduction to this subject see Robert Ornstein, "The Split and the Whole Brain," *Human Nature*, May 1978, pp. 76-83; Vadim L. Deglin, "Our Split Brain," *The Unesco Courier*, January 1976, pp. 4-32; John A. Taylor, "Progeny of Programmers: Evangelical Religion and the Television Age," *The Christian Century*, April 20, 1977, pp. 379-82; Douglass Cater, "The Intellectual in Videoland," *Saturday Review*, May

31, 1975, pp. 12-16; Robert J. Trotter, "The Other Hemisphere," *Science News*, April 3, 1976, pp. 218-23; Robert Ornstein, *The Psychology of Consciousness* (New York: Harcourt Brace Jovanovich, 1977); James B. Ashbrook and Paul W. Walaskay, *Christianity for Pious Skeptics* (Nashville: Abingdon, 1977); and Julian Jaynes, *The Origin of Consciousness in the Breakdown of the Bicameral Mind* (Boston: Houghton Mifflin, 1976).

CHAPTER 6

1. Charles H. Cooley, *Social Process* (New York: Charles Scribner's Sons, 1918).
2. From material in James Dahir, *The Neighborhood Unit Plan, Its Spread and Acceptance* (New York: Russell Sage Foundation, 1947).
3. For a pioneering critique of the concept see Svend Riemar, "Hidden Dimensions of Neighborhood Planning," *Land Economics*, May 1950, pp. 196-200.
4. For two excellent introductions to the research in this area see Suzanne Kellar, *The Urban Neighborhood* (New York: Random House, 1968); and Bender, *Community and Social Change in America*.
5. For the definitive statement on the homogeneous unit concept see C. Peter Wagner, *Our Kind of People: The Ethical Dimension of Church Growth in America* (Richmond: John Knox Press, 1978).

CHAPTER 7

1. For three versions of a more active leadership role now being advocated for pastors, see E. Mansell Pattison, *Pastor and Parish: A System Approach* (Philadelphia: Fortress Press, 1977); C. Peter Wagner, *Your Church Can Grow* (Glendale, Calif.: Regal, 1976), ch. 4; James D. Anderson and Ezra Earl Jones, *The Management of Ministry* (New York: Harper & Row, 1978), chs. 5 and 9; and Ezra Earl Jones and Robert L. Wilson, *What's Ahead for Old First Church?* (New York: Harper & Row, 1974), pp. 68-73.
2. Schaller, *Understanding Tomorrow* (Nashville: Abingdon, 1976), pp. 15-22.
3. In many denominations the pastor moderates the Session or chairs the Church Council or chairs the nominating committee or has absolute control over who will preach from that pulpit or is identified as the Pastor-in-Charge or has responsibilities which give the pastor either complete or dominant control over that aspect of ministry.
4. For an elaboration of the implications of this concept see Lyle E. Schaller and Charles A. Tidwell, *Creative Church Administration* (Nashville: Abingdon, 1975), pp. 38-44.